LOVE YOUR JOURNEY!

Have your Journey!
Enjoy

THE Ultimate Employee Guide

FOUNDEROLOGY

Succeed with Any Boss in Any Workplace

Find Your Sanity
Embrace Your Genius
Love Your Journey

THE Ultimate Employee Guide

FOUNDEROLOGY

Succeed with Any Boss in Any Workplace

Find Your Sanity
Embrace Your Genius
Love Your Journey

KATHLEEN WOOD

Founderology

COPYRIGHT © 2021 by

Kathleen Wood

Published by Soar 2 Success Publishing
Soar2SuccessPublishing.com

Printed in the United States of America
ISBN: 9781956465013

Back Cover Photo by
Jen Schildgen at *bluevervestudio.com*

Image on page 32
Credit to Shutterstock desdemona72

Image on page 53
Credit to Shutterstock Tridsanu Thopet

Table Of Contents

Dedication

**With gratitude, I dedicate *Founderology*
to all the Employees
who work with Founders to make
their visions a reality!**

Foreword

BY JAMIE GRIFFIN

Founder of Consult to Grow, Mentee & Recovering Employee

If you are a frustrated and confused Employee trying to succeed in working for a Founder, finding *Founderology* is the universe conspiring in your favor. In your hands is a powerful collection of stories, lessons, and practices that, when used, will allow you to thrive and succeed with any boss in any workplace.

Kathleen Wood and I met in the early 2000s when she was the business growth consultant for the entrepreneurial company where I began my career. Back then, Kathleen would visit our business monthly to check in, keep us aligned to prioritized strategies, and coach members of the team to build a solid business foundation for growth.

MEETING KATHLEEN

My first interaction with Kathleen was in the "office" at about 2 a.m. when she stumbled upon me working late on a strategy to find and hire Employees for new locations. I put the word "office" in quotes because the "office" was in an old house where if we used the breakroom microwave and toaster oven at the same time, we might trip the electrical breaker that was on the same circuit as the server room. This was before all our documents lived in the Cloud, so the words "Save your work!" were frequently yelled around lunchtime.

From the moment I met Kathleen, I knew she was a talented growth strategist and advisor. I felt then, and continue to feel, fortunate for her presence in my work and life. Kathleen has many gifts, but her abilities to directly connect with you, see through mental clutter to focus your attention where it matters most, and then inspire and motivate you to fully realize your capabilities are some of her most valuable. Kathleen also has more energy than anyone I've ever met in my life, and it is infectious to everyone around her.

SURVIVING A CRISIS

Five years after that first meeting, Kathleen joined the executive team of our company just in time to help our Founder and CEO navigate the complexities of going through and surviving Hurricane Katrina. A crisis, as you may have recently experienced with the COVID Pandemic, has an interesting way of accentuating both the *positive* and *negative*.

The positive might look like walking into a conference room at work forty-eight hours after a large Category Five hurricane made landfall and shuttered your business. When you walk in, you find all your coworkers in attendance, standing, ready to help the company restore operations despite lacking essential utilities.

The negative might look like working twenty-plus hour days, seven days a week, to the point of exhaustion that diminishes the quality of your work. It might look like continuing to work through confusion, misinformation, and doubt, in addition to watching leadership struggle to balance the risks of saving lives versus livelihoods.

Kathleen, side by side with our Founder, guided us through that pivotal moment that could have totally shuttered our business and ended our Founder's dream. She helped the Founder pursue progress over perfection. She guided the team to better clarity and cadence of communication. She helped save our business. The lessons from that time are expertly shared in the pages that follow, especially in Chapter 10: The Epicenter of Crisis.

In every career crisis, Kathleen has always been my go-to mentor and fixer. In every instance, Kathleen's stories, practices, and how and whys changed my perspective, allowing me to continue forward with greater clarity and less suffering. We have cried and laughed many times over workplace issues! I suspect you, too, will cry and laugh as you read this book, seeing yourself and unlocking your greatest potential in the chapters ahead.

WHY *FOUNDEROLOGY?*

Kathleen has advised hundreds of companies, which is significant to you because she's coached hundreds of Founders and thousands of Employees just like us. In this book, Kathleen takes the decades of wisdom she's gathered through thousands of professional coaching relationships. She gifts it to you to minimize your suffering and maximize your achievements.

Founderology is essential reading for any Employee looking to Find Your Sanity, Embrace Your Genius, and Love Your Journey of working with a Founder to make their vision a reality. Kathleen's relatable advice and thought-provoking ideas make this book the ultimate prescription for success with any Founder in any workplace.

Founderology 101

Founder
/foun-der/
Founder is used throughout this book as a term to capture the collective of Founders, Entrepreneurs, Business Leaders, Business Owners, Owner-Operators, Franchisors, and Franchisee-led businesses. *It's a title that encapsulates leaders with an entrepreneurial mindset in any workplace.*

Founderology
/foun-der-ol-uh-jee/
The Best Practices to Succeed with
Any Boss in Any Workplace.
The Ultimate Employee Guide to Find Your Sanity, Embrace Your Genius, and Love Your Journey of working with Founders. The suffix-*ology*, meaning the study of a specific area, comes from the Greek language.

THE *FOUNDEROLOGY* FRAMEWORK

There are many books written for Founders on how to succeed, win, grow and become the next great brand. There has never been a book written for Employees about how to succeed, win, and grow while working with a Founder—until now. *Founderology* is the first book to focus on how Employees can positively and productively maximize their opportunity and success when working with a Founder.

I believe that Employees just like you are the MVPs (Most Valuable Players) in any Founder's or business's success. I have been a growth strategist working with Founders and Employees to transform small companies into big businesses for over twenty years. I have had thousands of conversations with Employees and Founders as we have worked together charting the path of transforming small companies into big businesses.

Though the companies have all been uniquely different, the themes of the conversations with Employees have been very similar. Themes like: How do I gain a better understanding of my Founder? How do I improve our communication? How can I increase my performance and results, as my Founder never seems satisfied? How can I be part of creating a culture/workplace where everyone can thrive, and how can I proactively grow our business for the greatest productivity and profitability possible?

I knew if I could share valuable lessons and practices from these conversations that have supported and accelerated so many Employees' success, magic would happen. Magic I have seen time and time again as I have consulted and collaborated with Employees and Founders. The magic of transforming a Founder's vision to reality through

How can I
INCREASE MY
PERFORMANCE
AND RESULTS,
as my Founder
NEVER SEEMS
SATISFIED?

clarity, alignment, and a shared understanding between Employees and Founders.

When there is shared clarity, alignment, and understanding between Employees and Founders, this magic makes things happen. The impossible becomes possible. The ability to achieve things that no one thought was possible suddenly becomes a reality. It creates a culture of camaraderie and determination for Employees and Founders to be clear and aligned on a shared direction of taking their company and building it into a market leader, industry-award winner, and, in many cases, billion-dollar brands.

Founderology is filled with real-life lessons, practical advice, and success practices for you to grow and accel in a Founder-led business. As I thought about all these success practices, I realized I could write volumes of them. I wanted to focus on the ten most valuable success practices for how to work with any Founder in any workplace. I am confident that these ten success practices will be powerful for you, because Employees just like you have been helped by them too!

In *Founderology*, you will find my direct and insightful real-life how-to guide for you to better understand and gain perspective on how to:
- Understand the mindset of Founders and leverage it to support your success
- Stop wasting time trying to figure Founders out;

instead, stretch, grow, and thrive in a Founder-led business

🎧 Love your journey of working in the dynamic and ever-changing world of transforming a Founder's vision into reality

I have developed an easy-to-follow how-to framework to maximize the understanding and application of each success practice. As you understand and apply these success practices, they will create positive momentum for you.

Founderology Framework:

1. ***Founderology* Reality** — Situations, Scenarios, and Stories
2. **Find Your Sanity**— Understanding a Founder's Mindset
3. **Embrace Your Genius**—Your Opportunity to Thrive
4. **Love Your Journey -** Stop and Start Tips for Success
5. **Woodism**— Kathleen Wood's Version of Pearls of Wisdom

Why do Founders start and lead businesses? The simplest answer is they have an unwavering belief in the power of their vision to change the world. Many people will call them crazy. Yet, as we have seen throughout the history of business, Founders are just crazy enough to actually change the world. You, at this very amazing moment in your career, can be a part of changing the world too. Here is the secret in the Founder's sauce of success: no Founder can do it alone. They must have Employees just like you who get them and can grow with them.

I believe working with Founders is a rare and special career opportunity. The specialness and uniqueness of it can be lost if you don't know how to succeed with any Founder in any workplace. It is a completely different experience than any other job you may ever have in your career. I do know this and have said it a million times: working with a Founder is a true career gift. If this is your opportunity to work with a Founder, then please use everything in *Founderology* to learn, grow, thrive, and succeed!

I welcome you to the exciting world of *Founderology!*

Founder's Ego: "We" versus "Me"

The Healthier the Founder's Ego,
the Healthier the Employee's Ego

FOUNDEROLOGY REALITY

The big night had finally arrived. The entire team had been looking forward to this moment for a long time. The stage was set for an epic gala evening at the prestigious Best of Business Awards Ceremony. After many long, tireless months, missed holidays, skipped family and friends' events, and the toll of strained relationships, the team was more than ready to celebrate. They were primed to toast and enjoy their well-deserved recognition. Finally, the team's collective efforts of blood, sweat, and tears were being recognized as one of the nation's best new businesses.

The large audience buzzed with anticipation leading up to the presentation of the final grand award of the evening. Finally, the company's name was announced, and the Founder's name immediately followed. The crowd exploded in a roar of applause as the background music rose to a crescendo. The Founder slowly walked to the podium, smiling and waving to the crowd as the team stood up cheering, some even crying tears of joy. This recognition was the Founder and Employees' moment, to rejoice in all their much-deserved glory and success. All their years of sacrifice were immediately validated in this celebratory moment.

As the Founder quieted the crowd and began their acceptance speech, the team, beaming with pride, sat back down in their chairs. The Founder started to share the journey of the company's success, how hard the Founder personally had worked to get to this point, the many sacrifices the Founder made, from all the missed personal events to the strain on the Founder's family and friends. The more the Founder shared the story, the more the story became about one person and one person alone. The Founder.

Minutes into the speech, the Founder's story had completely transformed into being solely about the Founder and no one else. The Founder failed to acknowledge anyone on the team. The crowd sat in silence, mesmerized and inspired by the Founder's tenacity, resiliency, and grit. They hung on to every word the Founder shared about overcoming adversity to achieve award-winning success.

While the crowd was being inspired, the team slumped in their chairs. What had started as an evening of joyful smiles and tears had quickly turned to frowns of displeasure and tears of frustration. The team sat in confusion and disbelief as the Founder shifted the story of the business's success from "we" (the team) to "me" (the Founder).

Upon the conclusion of the Founder's speech, the audience rose to their feet and erupted in applause, all except for the team, who sat dumbfounded in utter and complete silence. During the post-event celebration dinner, the Founder was full of pride and excitement, while the team put their best "corporate" faces on to not let the Founder know the depths of betrayal they all collectively felt. Later, the Founder cluelessly asked the limo driver after the event, "Why isn't the team as happy as me?"

"WTF," the team kept repeating as they gathered at a local bar after the awards ceremony to blow off steam with rounds of shots. "How could the Founder have forgotten us, our contributions, and all of our sacrifices? We were there too!"

FIND YOUR SANITY

Over the next year, many of the original Employees left the company. In leaving, each Employee explained that they had accomplished everything they had wanted to do at the company and were grateful for the opportunity. While the Founder continued to give speeches, interviews, podcasts, and share their personal inspirational story of success, one by one, key original Employees left the company.

The Founder accepted each departure as a natural course of business. From the Founder's perspective, with their business's newfound success, it created opportunities to bring on new, fresh talent to keep their business vibrant and thriving. The Founder continued to be unaware of the impact of their initial awards acceptance speech and the many after until the last Employee from the original team resigned. In the final exit interview, the Employee asked the Founder, "Do you know why everyone has left?"

The Founder replied, "Yeah, they all got better offers."

"Well, that's the easy answer you accepted," said the Employee. "With all due respect, the real answer is, you made them invisible on the awards ceremony night when you essentially took credit for everything the team had achieved. You kept going on and on about your journey without once acknowledging the team of dedicated Employees who worked tirelessly to get you there."

The Employee continued, "Since then, you continued to keep the team invisible until they were all gone. A simple acknowledgment of the team that night would have gone a long way." The Founder sat quietly in disbelief, thinking, how many opportunities did I give everyone? How much money did they all make? I set their careers up for life, and everyone is enjoying a good life because of me.

Nonetheless, the Founder said nothing in return except to thank the Employee for their courage to share those comments. The Founder continued to lead with a "me first" ego and an attitude that Employees would come and go. Over the years, many great people did exactly that— they came and went through the company. The company did well, yet never achieved all of its potential. The original team always wondered why the Founder flipped the script from "we" to "me," and where the company would be if the Founder had never flipped.

DIFFERENTIATING THE "WE" VERSUS "ME"

In a Founder-led company, Employees and the Founder are all a "We" until the "We" becomes "Me," the point when the Founder makes a conscious or unconscious shift to separate from the team. Once the shift occurs, it is permanent and forever. For Employees, this can feel like the Founder moves forward in the spotlight while the team stays working in the shadows.

The spotlight shift can happen at any stage of a business, from a start-up to a well-established company. It occurs most frequently in Founder-led companies as they grow and receive external recognition. The spotlight only shines in one direction and on one person—the Founder.

As a dedicated Employee, how do you move forward after your heart gets broken when you discover that your seemingly amazing, larger-than-life superhero Founder is only human after all? When you find out everything you believed in about the Founder is wrong, and all the sacrifices you made to achieve success for the business—like the missed events, the excuses to family and friends about not showing up for important moments because of "critical" deadlines—now seem for nothing. When suddenly, you realize the story never was about you; it has always been about the Founder. For Employees, this is the realization that your Founder has broken your spirit, and for some, their hearts can lead to responses ranging from rage to utter despair to a desire to reset their priorities for a healthier life.

Employees begin asking themselves: "How did I miss it?" "How could I have been so blind, stupid, and naïve?" This disbelief only serves to make you more aggravated, and the questions compound: "When did my Founder become a narcissist, a spotlight grabber, or a solo artist?" "When did they forget about the 'we' and begin to focus on themselves?"

There is a great saying: "Never forget where you came from." Many Founders believe this a reminder to stay grounded and humbled as they climb the uphill battle to success. While it is an important reminder to stay grounded, I think it misses a massive point—it doesn't consider other people. I always suggest expanding that

"NEVER FORGET
where you
CAME FROM,
and NEVER FORGET
the people
WHO GOT
YOU THERE."

saying to be, "Never forget where you came from and never forget the people who got you here." This serves as a reminder that "me" is part of the "we" mindset. Imagine if the Founder accepting the award in the story would have operated from this belief.

What if the Founder had said, "I have never forgotten where I came from, and I will never forget the people who have helped me achieve so much success. I am so very grateful for every Employee who has worked tirelessly to make my vision a reality. Many of them are here tonight. Let me take a moment now to recognize them." Wow! Talk about building a lifetime of loyalty by publicly acknowledging the Employees.

The Founder's shift from "we" to "me" cuts to the core of an Employee's existence. It can rock your world in such a profound way that for many Employees, it changes their career trajectory, so they never again work for another Founder. On the other hand, some Employees will continue to work for their existing Founder. However, they may no longer be 100 percent committed, or at the very least, they will establish specific boundaries for their time. They will remain enthusiastic about their job and work extraordinarily hard, yet they will never again put their Founder's drive for success over their standards, happiness, or loved ones.

The Founder's shift almost immediately transforms loyal, dedicated, and committed Employees who were willing to run through walls for the Founder into Employees who now are just working hard at a job. It's not to say that this is a good or bad thing; it's just that shifts happen with Founders.

FOUNDERS AND EGO

As much as a Founder can seem like a superhero, they are still human and have egos like the rest of us. I find it funny when someone tells me they don't have an ego. Stating this only serves as a further acknowledgment that their ego exists. Egos are powerful forces. Most Founders have healthy and strong egos. A healthy ego is a key ingredient in a Founder's equation for success. A healthy ego helps a Founder navigate the roller coaster ride of being a Founder. It protects them when they get knocked down from rejection, failure, or the brink of devastation. It pushes the Founder when the business is moving forward productively and profitably.

For many Founders, seeing their names all over social media, written on billboards, and having millions of social followers is a very heady experience. Any person, much less a Founder, would be hard-pressed not to let some of it go to their heads. When a Founder's ego goes unchecked, the healthy ego becomes unhealthy—this is when the "we" transforms into "me."

Let's look at some comparisons between a Founder's healthy ego versus an unhealthy ego.

Healthy Ego	Unhealthy Ego
Asks questions	Stops asking questions
Seeks to understand	Stops seeking input
Is open to feedback	Ignores feedback/data
Builds a diverse team	Is surrounded by "YES" people
Encourages discussion	Uses power to shut people down
Focuses on outcomes	Must win everything
Relates to everyone on the team	Loses touch with reality
Believes healthy disagreements are acceptable	Believes all opposition is bad
Builds the team	Does their own thing
It is all about "we"	It is all about "me"

Psychologists, sociologists, behavioral specialists, and other professionals have studied the notion of ego for centuries. There is certainly no shortage of information about the ego. My intent for presenting the Founder's ego is about providing perspective so you can be better informed, more aware, and prepared to find sanity with your Founder, particularly with a Founder who seems to display attributes of an unhealthy ego.

Founders come in all shapes and sizes, and so do their egos. Having a better understanding of the Founder's ego through the lens of "healthy" and "unhealthy" can help you better navigate all the egos you encounter in business, including those of fellow Employees and your Founder.

Healthy Ego

As a Growth Strategist, I have worked with many Founders who started very humbly as we began to transform their small companies into big, very successful companies. In the beginning, many of the Founders were incredibly proud of their businesses and carried a great deal of pressure for ensuring their growth and financial viability.

Some of the Founders I worked with had businesses that were in rough shape financially, operationally, or suffering from a lack of quality leadership. They needed help yet did not know how to develop their paths to prosperity and success. These Founders were in pain and needed a new way forward. As we worked together, they gained more financial success, public recognition, and created great opportunities that positively changed their lifestyles, houses, cars, and vacations. What I was always impressed by was, no matter how successful these Founders became, many remained humble and continued to balance their healthy ego and humility with their success.

Many successful Founders have led, grown, and built successful businesses and teams with exceptionally healthy egos. Founders with healthy egos tend to exemplify a leadership style known as "servant leaders." They are those who serve a "higher calling," such as growing and supporting the well-being of the people and communities they belong to and serve. Servant leaders tend to put the needs of others first and help people develop to their highest potential. They drive to do well by doing good. Their success is the success of the team.

Servant leaders are often dismissed for being idealistic, weak, or small-thinking when just the opposite is true. It takes great strength, stamina, and courage to put others before self, especially when the Founder has risked everything to make their dream a reality. A Founder who has successfully led their business with a healthy ego also receives the greatest gift of all—a legacy of leaders who continue to grow and lead successful enterprises that positively impact people, industries, and communities for lifetimes. I have had the privilege to work with many Founders whose Employees went on to start businesses and achieve great success!

Unhealthy Ego

Some Founders actually like that their business is in a continuous state of change. Much of the change can be linked to the Founder's ego, just not in a positive way. For these Founders, the ego eventually transforms and shifts to making everything about what the Founder wants, how much they want, and when they want it. Nothing is too big, flashy, or outrageous in their minds. All of this is about building a larger-than-life image, brand, or business. They soon become one of the "it" people—that person everyone wants to take pictures with, hang out with, and be associated with all the time. Everywhere the Founder goes, so goes an entourage of admiring fans.

In my experience, this process is gradual and doesn't happen immediately. Over time, the Founder's reality becomes distorted by their adoration from fans, the royal treatment people give them everywhere, and the perks of popularity they receive. It's an amazing ride, and, if a Founder is not well-grounded, the ego shifts from healthy and humble to unhealthy and self-centered. At the same time, Employees who continue to work for the Founder notice the changes and soon become targets for the Founder's unhealthy ego attacks.

As this shift occurs, other subtle behaviors begin showing, such as a growing intolerance for things that have no immediate benefit to the business or cost the business money (e.g., company lunches, celebrations, holiday parties). In these cases, Founders exhibit greater frustration when things don't go specifically their way, especially when they ask for it more than once. They are quick to pull the trigger on firing Employees who disagree with them or do not conform to their manner of doing things. They make demands of Employees to move faster, work harder, and dig deeper.

A classic move is when a Founder publicly scolds everyone for their lack of effort. Then, they get into their expensive car and drive to the mountains for a relaxing getaway. All the while, the Employees are perplexed, as they are literally and figuratively left in the Founder's dust, shaking their heads.

One of the principal factors in a Founders' ego shift to unhealthy is found in fear. From my experience, it all comes down to some type or form of fear. Fear is a topic that will come up frequently in *Founderology*. Let me be clear; I am not saying that Founders are afraid or scared, about what they are doing. In fact, Founders are the opposite in that they are great risk-takers. I am saying that fear will come up frequently for a Founder as it relates to losing or failing. It's that fear that drives or paralyzes a Founder, as you will begin to understand in reading *Founderology*.

As Founders see their vision becoming a reality and achieve everything they have ever dreamed of, they may fear success. With success comes a deep-seated fear of potential loss of status, position, money, lifestyle choices, or anything else they have come to enjoy. In addition, they may fear being called out as a fraud. Other fears come into play, as well. For example, there may be a fear of clients or key Employees abandoning them. Perhaps there is a fear of broken relationships with close family members or friends because of the increasing demands of the job.

Another concern is that people will find out they are human, after all, and not a superhuman rockstar of business. Finally, facing themselves in the mirror if they lose everything can be overwhelming. All these fears compound, and the unhealthy ego starts to emerge. This shift in ego is sometimes the Founder's journey. Unfortunately, it becomes part of your journey, too.

NAVIGATING AN UNHEALTHY EGO

Will all Founders develop unhealthy egos? Certainly not. History continues to provide examples daily of Founders with healthy egos. Learn the lessons from working with Founders with healthy egos. Move forward in your career, mastering the balance between a healthy ego and accelerating the success of a business.

Here are a few action steps you can take when you work with a Founder who has an unhealthy ego:

- ☺ Accept that your Founder's unhealthy ego is ultimately their business driver. No matter what the vision statement posters state, it does not mean you are doomed and should quit your job. It just means you need to accept this is how your workplace operates.
- ☺ Learn to find your leadership voice and speak up against inappropriate behavior. I always suggest respectful delivery of messages to a Founder with an unhealthy ego. Always do remember that everyone is replaceable at some point in the journey.
- ☺ Recognize that if the Founder forgets about your contributions, you don't have to forget about your contributions. Keep driving forward and use this opportunity to build your capabilities, competencies, and career path.
- ☺ Learn lessons from a Founder with an unhealthy ego and try not to become that type of leader in the future.

EMBRACE YOUR GENIUS

STEPPING INTO YOUR GREATNESS

Working with a Founder will also affect your ego. As much as you want the Founder to maintain a healthy ego, you also have the opportunity to maintain a healthy ego. As I said at the beginning of this book, working with a Founder is one of the most memorable experiences you will ever have in your career, until, perhaps, one day when you are a Founder. Whether healthy or unhealthy, a Founder's ego provides you with an extraordinary gift—the gift of stepping into your greatness.

A Founder with a healthy ego will see more of your potential in terms of drive, capabilities, and competencies than you may see in yourself. They will encourage, motivate, inspire, and stretch you to rise and be more than you thought yourself capable of being. Believe in your Founder and yourself.

A Founder with an unhealthy ego provides you with another opportunity to find your own "leadership voice," to learn how to speak up for yourself, promote yourself, and participate in discussions with confidence and courage. Remember to be respectful, and you may even earn the respect of your Founder too!

Founders' egos are not the enemy, the devil, or the driver of destruction. However, they are part of everyone's career journey and an essential part of your professional (and personal) journey towards becoming wiser, healthier, and more self-aware.

Here are a few ways both Founders and Employees can keep healthy egos:

- Follow the Golden Rule: act toward others as you would want them to act toward you.
- It's *okay* to be a big shot; just don't act that way.
- Acknowledge when you do not know something, or ask for support or help.
- Take feedback as useful professional development, not as a personal criticism.
- Agree to disagree—the Founder and Employee are not always going to get along every day. However, agreeing to disagree opens options to move forward without resentment.
- Be human—recognize we all have the right to change and respect that right in both others and yourself.

The great salesman and motivational speaker Zig Ziglar once said, "Your attitude determines your altitude." That means having a positive attitude lifts your altitude above an unhealthy ego. A negative attitude pulls your altitude down to the level of an unhealthy ego. Think about your attitude. Does it pick you up and inspire you, or are you being pulled down?

It's amazing how our thoughts can impact our reality. Here is a challenge for you: what would happen if you changed your attitude and stepped into the greatness of your healthy ego altitude?

Love Your Journey

Stop

- ❌ Getting caught up in drama caused by an unhealthy ego
- ❌ Wasting time and energy discussing how to change the Founder's unhealthy ego
- ❌ Discounting your contributions because you are more focused on how the Founder is busy promoting their contributions

Start

- ➤ Recognizing that Founders are human even when they appear larger than life
- ➤ Setting boundaries of what is acceptable and unacceptable so you can contribute at a high level without missing out on life
- ➤ Leading with a Servant Leadership mindset

WOODISM

"Your thoughts become your reality; choose healthy, positive, and productive thoughts for your success."

Insatiable Pursuit of Perfection

SUCCESS PRACTICE 2

Jump in and enjoy the ride.
Very few people ever get to work with Founders,
so don't spend your time trying to fit them into
your world.
Stretch and thrive in theirs.

FOUNDEROLOGY REALITY

The deadline for the next quarterly ad for the business is fast approaching. The Founder has a very clear vision for how they want the ad to look. The Founder repeatedly tells the Marketing Manager what they are looking for in the ad. The Founder provides the Marketing Manager with detailed directions for how the ad should look, feel, and position the business.

The next day, the Marketing Manager presents the completed ad to the Founder…and hears nothing but silence. The Founder resists the temptation to blow up at the Marketing Manager for not following their specific directions. Simultaneously, the Founder is trying to figure out the best way to tell the Marketing Manager that this is not even close to the vision. The Marketing Manager already knows by the Founder's sheer silence that the ad will not work.

Finally, the Founder breaks the uncomfortable silence, takes out a red pen, and begins writing all over the ad. The Founder adamantly tells the Marketing Manager what their vision is *again* and insists the Marketing Manager take better notes this time. At the end of the meeting, the Founder and Marketing Manager agree they have arrived at a shared vision.

The Marketing Manager takes all the feedback and begins to redesign the ad, bringing in more people from the marketing team to assist in its development. The next day the team completes the new ad, and everyone is super excited. They all agree it is much better than the last ad and is precisely what the Founder is looking for this time.

The Marketing Manager presents the new ad campaign to the Founder. Again, the Marketing Manager is met with deafening silence. The Founder is thinking this ad is just not working. The Founder continues to look at it and thinks the Marketing Manager will never get it right. The Founder is suddenly struck with a new idea—perhaps an even better idea than the first ad.

The Founder takes out their red pen and begins to sketch out a new ad for the Marketing Manager. The Founder barks at the Marketing Manager, "Come on! Let's see some energy, and let's be taking notes." The Founder is energized and excited about this new direction. Simultaneously, the Marketing Manager lets out a sigh of frustration and exhaustion.

The Marketing Manager wonders while walking back to their desk if all this effort is worth it for just one ad. Doesn't the Founder know how many other priorities must be addressed? Doesn't the Founder realize that it is now one week before the campaign launch? Now they have to start over after wasting all this time.

The Marketing Manager goes back to the team and announces that they need to start all over. The Employees let out a collective sigh. "Not again," they comment. "Why doesn't the Founder just design the damn ad? We are never going to get it right!"

FIND YOUR SANITY

FOUNDERS' SCALE OF EMPLOYEE PERFORMANCE EXPECTATIONS

Founders have an uncanny ability to see their vision with crystal-clear clarity. This crystal-clear clarity leads Founders to the "insatiable pursuit of perfection." Meaning they never stop thinking about how or what needs to happen to make their vision a reality. There are many examples of how the insatiable pursuit of perfection plays out every day in a Founder-led business. This insatiable pursuit of perfection is especially frustrating for Employees. I have spent a lot of time explaining how this insatiable pursuit of perfection manifests into the never-ending "write–rewrite spiral." The *Founderology* Reality showcases how the "write–rewrite spiral" can play out on pretty much any topic or project.

Very little is superficial with a Founder. To some Employees, this could look and feel like endless perfectionism. However, for Founders, it's just part of how they make the visions in their mind a reality in their business. Founders are continuously in a perpetual state of evolving their visions, aligning them with their reality of business success and growth. As you sleep at night, Founders are awake, continuing to push their visions forward into reality.

Think about this: Do you work with a Founder who has very specific standards, is obsessively detail-oriented, or has other characteristics that could be defined as obsessive or compulsive? Have you ever asked why the Founder was so particular, specific, or insistent on everything being perfect? Or have you ever questioned your skills, competencies, or if you will ever be right? If you have answered "yes" to any of these questions, please know you are not alone. Understanding how a Founder is wired and how that impacts their expectations will support you in dealing with a Founder's insatiable pursuit of perfection.

FOUNDERS' WIRING AND CAPACITY

There are two crucial parts for you to learn relative to Founders' insatiable pursuit of perfection. The two parts are Founder Wiring and their Expectation Capacity. The combination of both parts provides great insights into how Founders think and why the perception of their actions and behaviors are not always easily understood. Even though each part is presented separately, please know they are intimately intertwined with each other. In fact, many would say they are codependent.

FOUNDER WIRING

The insatiable pursuit of perfection is a common denominator of Founders, and it is frequently misunderstood by most Employees. One element of this misunderstanding found in the difference between a Founder's wiring and an Employee's wiring. The matrix below highlights the differences.

Founder's Wiring	Employee's Wiring
Sees something no one else can see	Sees more directly in front of them
Focuses on possibilities	Focuses on practicalities
Talks about *why*	Talks about *how*
Has relentless energy	Is energetic
Finds inspiration everywhere	Looks to be inspired
Is motivated by vision and naysayers	Is motivated by personal achievements

There is no right or wrong in the above. It is what it is. However, it is important to understand that, at the very core, a Founder is wired differently. Founders do not see it as their responsibility to explain their wiring, their wiring differences, their work style, or to fit in.

It is equally important for Employees to avoid spending time trying to change the wiring of Founders. It is counter-productive to try to reconfigure or rationalize a Founder's wiring. Forget wondering why they are not more like everyone else or insisting they change their wiring for the greater good of everyone else. If Founders wanted to change, they would. There is nothing deep about it; they simply are not wired to be an Employee—they are wired as a Founder.

EMBRACE YOUR GENIUS

STRETCHING YOUR WIRING

No matter what your wiring is as an Employee—typical, atypical, strategic, analytical, technical, etc.—when you better understand your differences from the wiring of a Founder, an amazing opportunity occurs for you to better connect with your Founder, align with them, and accel.

Here are a few actions you can take to align and strengthen your own wiring with a Founder:

One action is to take a step back from the situation and do a quick analysis of the gap between what you see and what the Founder sees. Think about how big or small the gap is between your collective realities. Sometimes, closing the gap will require you to make an adjustment of perspective to gain greater alignment.

Struggling to find alignment can be very frustrating. It can also be challenging to think about ways to find alignment. One action you can take is to find proactive ways to gain greater understanding and alignment with the Founder's vision. This can include asking questions of the Founder and other team members for clarity of direction, insights into the company's vision, expectations for outcomes, and the list goes on. Seeking clarity always leads to achieving greater alignment.

Many Founders may not be able to articulate their full visions, as they are always continuously evolving them. If your current project or assignment is not mission-critical, it can be easiest for you to accept where the Founder's current vision is and find ways to support it until more is revealed later. As opposed to being unnecessarily frustrated by not having a complete vision.

Another action I recommend is to manage your expectations to minimize your frustration. If you expect a Founder to have everything spelled out, buttoned-up, and perfectly articulated, you will forever be frustrated. One of the great benefits of managing your expectations is that it takes the pressure out of the situation. It allows you to deal with the present, let go of the past, and not worry about the future. In the process, you potentially create better alignment between yourself and a Founder, too. This allows you both to be more proactive, flexible, and productive—and far less frustrated.

Expectation Capacity

As you start to understand that Founders are wired differently, I am sure you will also realize that they behave differently. The most obvious way is around what I call "Expectation Capacity." Many Founders live by the adage, "Good is never good enough; we can always do better."

Founders give their 100 percent effort to everything, yet never realize that their personal 100 percent effort is the average person's 200 percent effort, meaning that an average person's 100 percent effort is simply 50 percent effort in the Founder's eyes. For a Founder, this is right on the edge of incompetence. The scale below is a perfect illustration of a Founder's capacity perception.

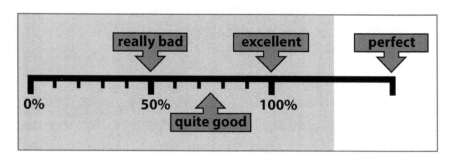

The impact is that the Expectation Capacity keeps Founders in a constant state of dissatisfaction and believing an Employee will never be able to achieve the Founder's vision. This state of dissatisfaction plays out in many ways. Here are a few of the classic ways dissatisfaction plays out in a Founder-led business:

- Nothing is ever good enough—even when one achieves amazing success.
- Big accomplishments are good for the moment, and then it is on to wanting more and even bigger accomplishments.
- Founders spend very little time to celebrations of successes or achievements because there is always more to do.
- Founders never stop and are always driving for more, even as people are failing and falling down around them.
- Founders are constantly looking for better people to fulfill their visions and at times disregard the current Employees making it happen.

It's not easy being the Founder some days. It's also not easy being an Employee some days. However, there are ways to make days easier for you.

Adjust Your Capacity

There are three coaching keys I share with all Employees to utilize in bridging forward progress with a Founder's insatiable pursuit of perfection. The first coaching key is to "seek clarity before taking action." Seek clarity with two very specific questions:

1. What are the specific deliverables for the ask, request, or assignment?

AND

2. What is the specific timeline for deliverables?

Often Employees will race to get a project or assignment done before asking these two important questions. The results are always the same: a fifty-fifty chance of being right on the deliverables and timeframes. These two questions significantly increase your probability of success. Founders are not big fans of being questioned on tiny details. However, they are big fans of great results. Clarity is the key to your success and theirs.

The second coaching key is for you to recognize that Founders' minds are always moving and evolving their visions. Founders tend to process through a perpetual state of ideation. This style of processing through ideation can be confusing. It can feel and look like a Founder has an idea today, and it's gone tomorrow. Compounding ideation even more is that Founders are often open to innovative ideas to enhance the ideation process.

An example of how the ideation process happens can be as simple as the Founder asking for a presentation. Yesterday, the presentation looked good. However, overnight, the Founder saw a different presentation, so now, the very next day, the presentation needs to be

FOUNDERS
are not big fans of
BEING QUESTIONED
on tiny details.
HOWEVER, THEY
are BIG fans of
GREAT RESULTS.

updated. After looking at the updated presentation, the Founder wants to make more tweaks, and the process of ideation continues.

Founders can also be verbal processors and will provide filtered and unfiltered feedback as part of the ideation process. Again, it is part of their ideation process to move everything closer to the vision in their mind's eye. My suggestion to you is to look at the feedback as part of the continuation of alignment and look for ways to incorporate their thinking into your work process. I always remind Employees, "It's not personal." It is truly about the Founder's ideation process to make their vision as close to perfection.

The third coaching key is this: if you want to develop as a valued Employee, make it a "game of alignment," and be in it to win it. When I work with Founders, I make a game out of how close I can align my vision to that of the Founders.

Every time I am closely aligned with their visions, expectations, and/or results, I take it as a win. Every time I am misaligned with their visions/expectations/results, I shift to get positively back into the game. This may include having more conversations, asking more questions, listening more intently, or seeking greater understanding. I know you and your fellow team members give it your heart and soul, bringing your best work and suggestions forward. As you are bringing your work forward, see it through the eyes of your Founder and anticipate their responses.

This is a great way to shift your expectations and perceptions away from how it makes you feel personally and make it a game of professional development.

Another simple and powerful version of the game, and equally easy to play, is to start counting the number of reworks, tweaks, changes, and evolutions. Challenge yourself to lower the number with all your work and efforts. When the number moves into single digits, you are truly making great progress for yourself, the Founder, the business, and the entire team. Be in it to win it and enjoy the game of alignment.

Love Your Journey

Stop

- ❌ Trying to change a Founder's wiring
- ❌ Being disappointed by the Founder's continuous feedback
- ❌ Taking the lack of a Founder's display of gratitude personally

START

❯ Embracing ideation as part of the Founder's process

❯ Recognizing that nothing is superficial with a Founder—everything matters

❯ Stretching yourself and your thinking to proactively align your wiring with the Founder's wiring

WOODISM

"Be in it to win for yourself; be open to all the possibilities of the journey!'

The Clash of Corporate Things

SUCCESS PRACTICE 3

The clearer the leader, the clearer the team.

FOUNDEROLOGY REALITY

Not long ago, a good friend who was an executive in a fast-growing company called me and asked, "Can you please talk to our Founder? Our Founder wants to discuss strategic planning with you." The Founder built their business to over $150 million in sales and wanted to accelerate its growth to $500 million in sales.

Upon meeting the Founder, I asked about their strategic planning methods. The Founder replied, "Kathleen, strategic planning is a waste of time. We have done strategic planning many times in the past, and it was all a waste of time. These types of 'corporate things' look good, and yet they very rarely deliver results. You need to understand we have many things going on in our business right now. As a result, we can only dedicate a half-day to developing a three-year strategic plan."

I provided my friend with an update about my conversation with the Founder. My friend started laughing, "How are we going to make all this planning happen in a half-day? In all seriousness, our team also needs clarity and a shared sense of direction from this planning session."

After more discussions, the CEO and I agreed to implement my accelerated strategic planning process that minimized the team's time and maximized the effectiveness of the strategic planning process. When we completed the strategic plan, the CEO was incredibly pleased with the results: a shared vision, clarity of direction, an aligned team, and a process for measuring results. Yes, it did take more than a half-day; however, over a short period of time, meeting intermittently and working collaboratively, the company, the team, and the CEO were transformed by the process. The trajectory of their business was also accelerated.

FIND YOUR SANITY

Founders are consistent when it comes to their perspectives on "corporate things." Corporate things can include strategic planning and organizational "pillars," such as visions, mission statements, written plans, and policies, just to name a few.

I am constantly asked why Founders have such disdain and disrespect for traditional business best practices known by Founders as corporate things. The simplest answer I can give is twofold, based upon my experiences:

- ⊛ Founders have a core belief that if the vision or plan is written down, it is the equivalent of being forever set in stone. Founders want the flexibility and freedom to change their minds, direction, or decisions without being cemented to corporate things.
- ⊛ Founders also tend to believe that corporate things create bureaucracies, and that is poison to a Founder's sense of freedom and flexibility.

CORPORATE THINGS AND WHY THEY MATTER: FOUNDERS AND CORPORATE CLASH

Some Founders believe that if they share their visions, their missions, and their written plans for all to see, they are going to be held accountable for everything written down. Founders don't want to be held back or positioned to be questioned by others on their visions and direction for achieving it. They don't want to be constrained. They want the freedom to change their minds. In fact, what they really want is complete control to change anything they want at any time.

Check out the differences between a Founder mindset and a corporate mindset relative to strategy, vision, mission, and written plans on the following page.

Founder Mindset	Corporate Mindset
"I have a plan in my mind."	A written plan helps the team see the direction.
"This is how I work."	We need policies and procedures.
"I know where we are going."	A vision statement inspires teams.
"Everyone needs to work hard."	Mission statement guides and builds team alignment.

Convincing Founders to develop these corporate things can be a real challenge for Employees. Many Founders believe that if the company does have a clear vision, mission, and written plan and the company fails, it will be because the Founder had the wrong vision or mission. Remember, Founders don't want to be wrong—or at least don't want to accept that they can make mistakes.

Think about this hypothetical example of a $100 million company with thousands of people working across hundreds of locations. Within this company, there is a complex supply chain, diverse constituencies, and layers upon layers of management, yet no one in the company clearly knows the company's vision or mission or has seen a written plan. All the team hears and understands from the Founder is "just get your damn job done."

I said, "hypothetical." You would hope this is not the case. Unfortunately, in truth, it happens more often than most Employees realize. It is astounding yet true that many

FOUNDERS
don't want to
BE WRONG
or at least don't want to
accept that they can
MAKE
MISTAKES.

Founder-led businesses operate like this daily. Imagine how much a business would achieve if teams had a clear vision, mission, and written plan—you know, corporate things.

As I continually explain to Founders and Employees, these are not simply corporate things, and they are not bad. They are tools for success, tools that create efficiency and effectiveness in helping Employees contribute and be successful in their jobs. These are excellent tools for Employees to capture the Founder's thought process for greater team alignment.

For as many advances we have made as humankind, Employees still cannot read a Founder's mind. Therefore, the Founder's mind needs to be brought to the team in the form of clear, well-crafted corporate things—vision, mission, and written plans, to mention a few. One saying I often share is: "People cannot follow a vision they cannot see."

EMBRACE YOUR GENIUS

WRITING THE PLAN YOURSELF

One major opportunity for Employees come when I have the discussion about breaking the invisible hierarchy. This is the long-held belief that prevents Employees from acting on their own, because the invisible hierarchy says they cannot. Who developed this invisible hierarchy? Who will stop you from taking the initiative and writing the plan, if not for the whole company, at least for your team?

I always ask teams of Employees, "What is stopping you from writing a plan, developing a timeline of deliverables, or even just setting goals?" The typical answer is, "We are waiting." You already know the answer—waiting on the Founder for the plan, because that's how the invisible hierarchy works from the top down.

Here are four simple steps you can take to develop your own plans and use them immediately in your workplace to thrive and break through the invisible hierarchy.

- 💡 Remember how most Founders ideate and verbally process? Here is your opportunity. Start writing down what they say as they are saying it. This is how Founders share their plans. If you can capture what the Founder is saying, you have the beginning of a written plan to share and align the Founder with the team.
- 💡 Ask the two key questions for clarity and aligning in discussions:
  - 💡 "What specific deliverables are you looking for?"
    AND
  - 💡 "What is your timeframe?"
- 💡 Draft a plan outline. Keep it simple and visual. Don't bog it down with too much narrative or details. Also, note that many Founders are also visual learners. Visuals can include things like PowerPoint presentations filled with charts,

flowcharts, bullet points, and so on. Think of it as preparing a visual executive summary.

💡 Share your plan outline with your Founder and ask for feedback relative to accuracy, alignment, and direction.

Will this always work out perfectly? Will there be some chaos when everyone starts writing plans? Will there be a need for a leader to step up or step in and coordinate planning? Yes, of course, all of this is true. However, will your Founder appreciate the initiative and results? Absolutely!

THE SIGNIFICANCE OF FOUNDER FREEDOM

Sadly, so many Founders miss the fact that by developing a vision, mission, and written plan, they gain what I call "Founder Freedom." This is the freedom for Founders to explore, innovate, and create because they are completely unencumbered by the constant need to provide hourly and daily direction while also making all decisions for the company. The daily grind of all these activities tends to wear down even the strongest of Founders and can create a lot of unnecessary drama. Implementing corporate things positively supports both the Founder and the Employee in finding the freedom to succeed and enjoy the journey.

Approaching a Founder who needs and would benefit from the use of some of these corporate things is best done by highlighting opportunities like better results, communication, and efficiency. All these areas are important to Founders. Here are a few tips I share with Employees to help Founders lessen their resistance to corporate things.

One tip is presenting corporate things as tools to make the team more efficient and more effective, rather than pointing out the Founder's inability to develop a plan. Take the initiative on the plan and share it with the Founder as a proposed direction and ask for feedback.

Another tip is to highlight your motivation, like, "We are not developing corporate things; we are working to increase the performance and the results of our team. Having a plan and clear directions would definitely help us move faster and more productively."

I have also worked with Founders who do not want their teams to have a written plan for many reasons, including lack of trust and multiple issues around giving people the entire plan. In these circumstances, my tip to Employees is to keep going back to the importance of having a plan for the team to accelerate the growth of the business. Maybe instead of asking for a three-year strategic plan, the ask could be for a quarterly plan to start a planning process.

Ultimately, I know for a fact, once a Founder realizes that having these corporate things in place is far better than keeping the company and everyone in it guessing about what's coming next, life becomes better for everyone. As many Employees have experienced through the years, when Founders provide and give clarity, everyone is amazed by how much less complicated their world becomes. It truly creates freedom for all.

LOVE YOUR JOURNEY

STOP

- ❌ Asking for a plan (it's useless)
- ❌ Waiting for a plan (it's not coming)
- ❌ Insisting Founders write things down (it's never going to happen; forget asking them to dictate either)

START

- ❯ Seeking ways to translate the Founder's vision to paper
- ❯ Proactively planning and asking the Founder for input
- ❯ Breaking the invisible hierarchy (its only purpose is to hold you back)

WOODISM
"Don't ask a unicorn to be a horse."

A Founder-Led Culture

CULTure=Clarity, Unity, Leadership, Team

FOUNDEROLOGY REALITY

Founder-led cultures have their own unique characteristics. To an Employee, a Founder-led company culture can feel a lot like, "Do as I say, not as I do." It boils down to what type of culture or unwritten rules are in place for the Founder and the Employees. Let's look at some real-life examples of Founder-led cultures.

EXAMPLE 1

The Founder stays out all night and does not attend the scheduled Managers' meeting at 8:00 a.m. the next morning. No one says anything, and the management team leaves frustrated. Many of the Employees who also were out late with the Founder still show up to the meeting. One Employee overslept, missed the early morning meeting, and receives a write-up for missing the meeting from Human Resources.

EXAMPLE 2

During the workday, the Founder leaves to attend to personal appointments, including a haircut, massage, drinks with friends at lunch, and going to their kid's middle-school soccer game during the afternoon. No Employee at work says anything, as all meetings, calls, and deadlines get rescheduled to later when the Founder returns to the office.

EXAMPLE 3

Several Employees start to take on the same behaviors as the Founder. When the Founder is ready for a team meeting, the Founder finds out key Employees are running personal errands. The Founder immediately insists that new policies are in place that prohibit Employees from using company time for personal errands.

EXAMPLE 4

The Employee takes off their first weekend in months and turns off their cell phone to enjoy their own over-the-top weekend without interruption. The Employee arrives at the office on Monday morning energized from the weekend, only to be told that they missed an important email that needed to be addressed ASAP, and now the entire business is in jeopardy. They also receive a lecture from the Founder on being selfish, being unavailable, and do they not understand how hard the Founder and the entire team are working? This happens even though the week before, the Founder went on vacation and never responded to any emails or phone calls.

There are thousands of examples of how cultural lines get blurred and distorted in a Founder-led business.

Find Your Sanity

The concept of a culture essentially captures the written and unwritten behaviors of an organization. A well-defined culture comes to life and action through corporate things such as purpose, vision, mission, and values. Culture can also capture specific business behaviors, like how Employees are respected, recognized, and rewarded.

Maybe you have heard these statements about culture?
- "Their culture is just like a family."
- "They have a winning culture."
- "They have an awesome culture."
- "Everyone in their culture is so committed."

Culture can also go in the opposite direction.
- "That place is toxic."
- "If you like politics, work there."
- "That's nothing but a good old boys club."

No matter how many times a Founder tells Employees, "We are all family," "We're all on the same team," "We're all in this together," or any other unifying statements, there is always an unspoken line between the Founder and Employee. You are all one team to the Founder—until you begin to act and behave like a Founder.

FOUNDER-LED CULTURE BY DEFAULT AND BY DESIGN

Many Founders create, define, and drive their company cultures by default versus by design. The early start-up stages of most companies have Founder-led cultures developed by default. Culture by default comes to life when Employees follow the actions, decision-making, and communication of the Founder. As Employees join the company, they learn the culture from what they see, hear, and experience from the Founder. Most of these key learnings are linked back to the Founder's behaviors.

Additionally, trying to succeed in a Founder-led culture is more difficult because the Founder is always changing the culture as they change their minds. Culture by default only works well for companies when they are just beginning.

As the company continues to grow, the Founder's focus starts to shift to building the business. As a result, the culture continues to grow by default. A culture created by default is good until it is no longer good. Think about culture like air.

Culture by default is how clean air becomes polluted. Like air, culture needs to be clear and defined, evolved, nurtured, and kept healthy at every growth stage. Air doesn't immediately go from excellent to poor; it happens gradually over time when it is not attended to or cared for consistently.

A Founder-led culture is also subject to changing air quality too. The early, fun-loving, competitive, "We are family, and no one is going to stop us," camaraderie culture modeled by the Founder can, over time, erode into a culture of polluted air.

| Polluted Air | Clean Air |

A Founder-led company where culture is defined by design builds a powerful foundation for a culture of clean air. Many Founders recognize the importance of culture and commit to developing it by design, intentionally defined by the Founder, and with the participation and input of Employees.

Culture by design is when the Founder has invested time and attention into a formal process to define purpose, mission, vision, and core values. It also includes developing and articulating how Employees will be respected, rewarded, and recognized. A vital element of culture by design is having a system for consistently measuring the health of the culture. This can include performance measurements from cultural surveys, feedback groups, and other tools to measure the culture's authenticity.

Several years ago, I participated in a leadership panel at a national conference. I was asked by an audience member, "How quickly could I change a company culture?" My answer was simple and confident: "I could change the culture in one day if I removed the leader." The audience gasped, and many raised their hands in objection, saying that was impossible. One of the best illustrations of this occurs when a Founder leaves a company, either voluntarily or involuntarily.

Everyone knows the culture changes the minute the Founder leaves the building. Depending on your relationship with the Founder, you typically know what that culture shift will mean to you and, in some cases, the company.

Company culture must be defined by design and evolve as the business grows. As I like to say, "Stay true to your cultural roots; however, be relevant to your changing world." Well-defined cultures can sustain through highly driven times, difficult times, and even in times of great crisis. As healthy cultures evolve, culture champions are created. Culture champions lead and nurture the culture as the business grows.

STAY TRUE
to your
CULTURAL ROOTS;
however,
BE RELEVANT
to your
CHANGING WORLD.

No Founder I have ever met has ever aspired to create a toxic work environment for their Employees. I am confident that having a toxic culture was never part of anyone's vision board for success. No Founder wakes up each morning saying, "Hey, I hope to create a work environment where all the Employees are completely miserable." I am equally confident Employees do not wake up every day saying, "Today is the day I am going to ruin my Founder's business once and for all." Most Founders want a healthy company culture, and they need your help in designing it and keeping it healthy.

FOUNDER-LED CULTURES AND YOU

Why is understanding a Founder-led culture essential for you to know? Or asked differently, how can you better understand your Founder-led culture and your ability to keep it healthy? Cultures exist because of the Founder and Employees in the company and the quality of the air they create. Your opportunity is to be aware of and support the quality of the air you are breathing. Is the air healthy and clean, or is it slightly polluted and you don't cough that much, or is it thoroughly polluted and so toxic that you literally can't even breathe? Sometimes it is hard to recognize the air quality until it's too late.

When I discuss Founder-led culture with Employees, I always start with the first four letters of culture, "CULT," which stands for Clarity, Unity, Leadership, Team. This is a model I like to share with Employees in Founder-led cultures to help them read their company's air quality. I have heard so many times that cults are bad, and there are definitely some bad ones for sure. In this instance, I am talking about the power of a good cult. Think about things like having a "cult-like" following of Employees, customers, or a community. When it comes to a healthy culture— there is only good in Clarity, Unity, Leadership, and Team.

Ask yourself the following questions to determine what type of air quality you have in your Founder-led culture:

Clarity— If a friend asked you to describe your work environment and how you felt every day going to work, what would you say?

Unity— How strong is the alignment between your Founder and the Employees? Do you have a shared vision of success or direction?

Leadership— How would you describe your Founder? Does your Founder say one thing and do something different time and time again? How does your Founder treat you?

Team— Does teamwork exist in your culture? Does everyone, for the most part, work together? Or, is the work environment competitive, with people working against each other to get ahead or be the Founder's favorite?

Your answers to these questions will help you understand your air quality. Positive responses indicate the air quality is good for you. Negative answers may show the air quality is not the best. Not having many answers would suggest that you have an excellent opportunity to ask your Founder and team more questions to learn more about the air quality.

THE UNSPOKEN LINE—SEPARATION OF CHURCH AND STATE

In a Founder-led culture, Founders and Employees often describe company culture as being like a "family"— "We're all a happy family," "Everyone treats everyone like family," and so on. Honestly, it is inspiring to hear about companies that refer to their cultures as "like a family." If you are completely honest with yourself, it is possible to say families are not always picture-perfect. All families have moments of challenge, conflict, distance, joy, love, happiness, and much more.

The same goes for a Founder-led company culture. It has all of the above. It also has another element not always found in families—what I call the "separation of church and state," to distinguish between the Founder (church) and the Employees (state). When you understand the unspoken line of separation between the Founder's idea of culture versus the company's stated culture, you can thrive between the lines. Let's look at some examples of how this concept of Founder/Employees (church/state) plays out in business on a day-to-day basis.

Founder (Church)	Employee (State)
"I may or may not show up for meetings."	"I have to be at all meetings."
"I will take off time when I need or want it."	"I have to request time off in advance."
"I will spend money as I want."	"I have a budget."
"I will persist until I get what I want."	"I have to collaborate and concede."
"I will work from my own rules."	"I have to follow our policies and procedures."

Many Employees will look at this table and say, "That's not a Founder-led culture; that's just a double-standard for everyone who works around here." The double-standard statement is valid. Employees get caught in the trap of believing that the Founder has created "a double-standard" performance, and Employees often spend so much time being upset over it. This double-standard assessment is spot-on once the culture of the company is polluted. In a healthy culture, although the double standard may not be as prevalent, the unspoken line between the Founder and Employee will still exist.

In the early stages of a company, there is a shared belief that everyone in the company is the same and has equal status. Only one person is being treated differently from all others, and it is the same person setting the standard, the Founder.

The Founder rarely sees a double standard. Instead, the Founder simply sees this as their right not to be held to the same standard as everyone else because they are the Founder. That's what the church and state metaphor is about; it clearly illustrates the unspoken line between how a Founder wants to behave and their expectations of how Employees should behave. It is the unspoken line that creates a separate and distinct difference between them.

No matter what the Founder may say about being a family-led culture, this unspoken line always exists. Your greatest opportunity is to accept the unspoken line and continue to grow between the lines.

EMBRACE YOUR GENIUS

SUCCEEDING IN A FOUNDER-LED CULTURE

There are many ways for Employees to find success in a Founder-led culture.

- In the early stages of a business, enjoy the ride; nothing else is quite like it.
- Recognize that culture is dynamic and ever-changing, especially in a Founder-driven business. Be aware of its air quality.
- Be an active voice in recognizing the signs when the "air quality" is changing. Understand that maintaining a healthy company culture is everyone's responsibility, not just the Founder's.

💡 In a polluted culture, you always have choices. Ask yourself, what is my willingness to continue to stay at the company? Will it diminish or empower me? How can I impact the air quality myself? It is your choice to make to be part of the solution.

What I love most about company culture is that it is the one element of business that can never be "stolen" by the competition. Culture is not possible to duplicate in any other business because it is unique to the Founder and Employees of each company. It is also one of the most significant and attractive elements for creating a company that Employees like you want to work at and contribute to every day.

A healthy culture is one where everyone achieves success together, and that makes for amazing air quality!

Love Your Journey

Stop
- ✘ Thinking you and the Founder are equals
- ✘ Behaving like the Founder and ignoring the unspoken line
- ✘ Criticizing the "double standard" that you believe exists

START

- ❯ Recognizing even in a Founder-Led company culture, it is still a business
- ❯ Following company policies and practices even if the Founder does not
- ❯ Being aware of the quality of the air you breathe in your company culture

WOODISM

"The only competitive differential in business is culture—create a CULT that inspires the best in everyone!"

The Energy Juice—
The Good, Bad, and Ugly
SUCCESS PRACTICE 5

Where the Founder focuses, the team focuses.
What you focus on will grow, whether it's good,
bad, or ugly. Choose your focus wisely!

FOUNDEROLOGY REALITY

Unfortunately, the origin of my "Founder Asshole" definition comes from actual experiences.

Founder Asshole
/**foun**-der as-(h)ōl/

When a Founder expresses displeasure with Employees
over the lack of perceived perfection with emotional
and abusive behaviors. These include personal
attacks, berating individuals, screaming, swearing,
and engaging in other extreme forms of verbal abuse.
These behaviors also include scheduling meetings at
ridiculous times of the day and night, texting people
incessantly, and insisting people be available to work
on all scheduled days off, vacations, and holidays.

One example of this definition was brought to life with a Founder who had zero tolerance for customer complaints. No matter how big or small, a customer complaint to the Founder was deemed a massive failure, even if the customer was in the wrong. The Founder's sensitivity about customer complaints was so intense that the Founder was im-mediately alerted by email if a complaint was received via email, phone, or posted on social media. The Founder's response to customer complaints were legendary regarding the Founder's brutality with the Managers and Employees.

The Founder would call the Manager, day or night, regardless of the hour, to find out the specifics of the complaint. The Founder then proceeded to verbally attack the Manager and all Employees involved in the complaint. The Founder insisted on taking disciplinary action against everyone involved. This included reducing hours and bonuses, and cutting the entire team out of all company activities until there was significant improvement or until the Founder had become distracted and was no longer mad at the team.

Time and time again, the Founder would show no remorse for their behaviors. They saw absolutely nothing wrong with sending all-night text messages and early morning voicemails, yelling and screaming at the Employees over one customer complaint.

The Employees learned to sit in silence while the Founder would rant on and on. They eventually would get upset and start telling the Founder about the thousands of happy customers before this one complaint. The Founder would immediately shut them down in a screaming rant because the Founder wanted to make sure that every Employee knew the focus was not on happy customers. The focus was on the one complaint.

Weeks after these outbursts of insanity, the Founder would talk about how they were committed to personally changing to prevent these outbursts of anger, yet the change would never come. Ultimately, everyone realized this was how the Founder was always going to behave. Thus, the definition of a Founder Asshole.

FIND YOUR SANITY

Time and again, we see how Founders are, by their very nature, highly driven in their journey to achieve their dreams of success. Being highly driven does not make a Founder good or bad. It is merely, once again, another part of their overall DNA. Highly driven Founders can achieve results in ways that many would never believe possible. There are times when highly driven Founders can shift into overdrive and become extreme, where never settling equates to zero room for error, no matter what. This overdrive brings out the good, bad, and ugly in Founders.

THE ENERGY JUICE— THE GOOD, BAD, AND UGLY

What fuels a Founder's drive is what I call "Energy Juice," to which nothing else compares. It is the adrenaline that propels the Founder to keep going even when they are tired, disillusioned, frustrated, overwhelmed, and even when they are achieving success. You cannot see the Founder's Energy Juice immediately. However, over time you will see it in their extreme behaviors.

Whether positive or negative, the Founder's Energy Juice is this extraordinary level of energetic fuel that plays out in extremes. What is important to understand is that as much as the world appreciates the brilliance of a highly driven Founder, there is always a ying to a yang. If brilliance is the ying, then a Founder's Energy Juice is the yang. They both exist in a Founder, and they both will impact you and the business, too.

Energy Juice can be good, bad, or ugly. No matter which of these it is, for a Founder, it is typically extreme. Energy Juice can manifest in positive behaviors, such as extreme workouts, extreme philanthropic initiatives, extreme reading, extreme spiritual practices, or extreme participation in external boards and associations. On the negative side, it can be extreme use of alcohol, drugs, or sex, verbal or physical abuse, or engaging in other illegal or immoral behaviors.

As crazy as it may seem, a crisis is the greatest source of Energy Juice for Founders, so much so that Founders will consciously and subconsciously create crises to kick start their Energy Juice. This includes activities like leaving the business with no direction or not making critical business decisions, yet refusing to let anyone else make decisions. It can also include sitting in meetings and being unemotional or incredibly disruptive. Sometimes the Energy Juice can be created by the Founder not engaging in any communication for days, weeks, or months, or behaving in a passive-aggressive manner toward everyone.

The Founder's Energy Juice is a subject area that very few Employees will discuss, yet most know all about it. Employees will name it as the Founder going through one of their "episodes" or "fades." Employees will be respectful and resilient as the Founder works through their so-called episode.

Over time, many Employees come to accept that this is just how the Founder operates. The matrix on the next page illustrates a top-line overview of the impact of Founder's Energy Juice on the relationship between the Founder and the Employee.

Good	Bad	Ugly
Extreme Positives	Extreme Negatives	Extreme Destruction
FOUNDER: Employees Need Extreme Personal Development	FOUNDER: Employees Need to Work at Extreme Levels of Performance	FOUNDER: Employee Performance is Extremely Disappointing
EMPLOYEE: The Founder is Highly Driven	EMPLOYEE: The Founder is Never Satisfied	EMPLOYEE: The Founder is an Asshole

GOOD GOES BAD—GOOD ENERGY JUICE

Here are a few examples of the extreme behaviors associated with Good Energy Juice that you might experience with a Founder: obsessive exercising, overinvolvement in philanthropic initiatives, nonstop reading, continuous spiritual practices, or participation in way too many external boards and associations. If you look closely, there is truly nothing wrong with any of the things listed except for when the Founder becomes consumed by it.

A great illustration of how Good Energy Juice impacts you is to look at an example many Founders utilize, obsessive exercising. One day, the Founder is doing a healthy forty-five-minute daily workout. The Founder starts to feel better, sees some results, and Employees start to comment on their improved appearance. The Founder increases their workout because now they want more results even faster than before. They increase their workout to two hours a day, decrease their food intake, and start looking at more ways to exercise during the day. They begin exercising morning, noon, and night.

Soon the Founder is having conversations with Human Resources about every Employee needing to be involved in an exercise program, and saying that exercise needs to be part of each meeting. Ultimately, the Founder takes the extreme position that all Employees need to be physically fit. The Founder's Good Energy Juice shifts to overdrive, and now everyone is going to get with the physical fit program immediately whether they want to or not. Good has definitely gone bad.

FOUNDER'S DESPAIR—BAD ENERGY JUICE

Founder's despair is when the Founder has simply lost their way in their business, or their life. They start to act out in extremes of self-sabotaging behaviors or periods of disconnection from the business. Life truly becomes a struggle, and despair starts to sink in. The business that once energized them is now dragging them down. This does happen to many Founders at different points in their business. The difference here is when it lasts longer than a brief period and becomes the Founder's way of life.

Sadly, there are also countless stories of Founders who did not make it back from the edge of despair. Founders always have a choice to get or ask for help. Unfortunately, for some Founders, when their despair goes unchecked, they can harm themselves or others. The choice of business over life is one that can be prevented when a Founder recognizes and acts upon the need for help.

Supporting Founders sometimes also means intervening to get them help. Thankfully, with help and support, many Founders can find their way out of despair and back to better days and a healthier lifestyle.

FOUNDER ASSHOLE—UGLY ENERGY JUICE

Founders can rationalize situations when success is not immediately achieved. They are tolerant when things don't always go the exact way they envisioned or planned. They can find the internal fortitude to rise to the occasion to overcome disappointment, frustration, and keep the grind moving forward. Clearly, Founder's Energy Juice, both good and bad, can help them in fueling forward movement.

However, there is one group of Founders whose expectations and demands are extreme and unrealistic. They are intolerant when things don't *go perfectly* their way. These Founders only have one name: "Founder Assholes." These are the Founders who object if any level of total perfection is not achieved. In their eyes, the team, the business, and, in some cases, the consultant have failed. These Founders are fueled by Ugly Energy Juice. Most of their actions and behaviors are unpleasant and unnecessary in today's workplace.

On more than one occasion, I have had the displeasure of working with Founder Assholes. Not for long, but even the best of us can get fooled. A Founder Asshole uses their position of power to act and treat Employees with extreme disrespect and abuse.

Founder Assholes get so outraged over the lack of perceived achievement that they will express it to their Employees with overboard emotional and abusive behaviors and by publicly humiliating Employees. Other behaviors can include scheduling meetings at ridiculous times of the day and night—5:00 a.m. in-person meetings, Thanksgiving morning meetings, or meetings at 10:00 p.m. on Friday night. Or, they are prone to other behaviors such as texting people incessantly and insisting people be available at any time of the day or night.

ARE YOU WORKING FOR A FOUNDER ASSHOLE OR A BRILLIANT GENIUS?

Here is a quick check to see if you are working with a Founder Asshole or a brilliant genius. There can be a fine line between them, and sometimes Employees rationalize that a Founder's brilliance is what drives them to be an Asshole. If you see or are experiencing these behaviors on a consistent basis, you are working with a Founder Asshole.

- Extreme standards that are impossible to achieve.
- Everyone and everything is disposable.
- There is no loyalty. Everyone can be replaced.

- ☻ There is no discrimination. Everyone is treated like crap.
- ☻ They believe it is their right to treat people any way they want to in order to get the job done.
- ☻ Founder Assholes typically have zero remorse for the damage they have inflicted upon others.

Look, let's be honest, there is absolutely 100 percent no judgment here. As I have worked with Employees, I have heard so many reasons why Employees work for Founder Assholes. Here are the top answers I typically hear:

- ☻ "It's an amazing opportunity to work with someone brilliant, even if that person is an Asshole."
- ☻ "I will never find a job that will pay me this much again."
- ☻ "It's not so bad, and you get used to it after a while because the Founder Asshole treats everyone the same."
- ☻ "If I make it through this, I will be able to write my ticket anywhere because I will be able to tell people I survived."

I have also witnessed people spending years of their lives missing key moments and memories of life because a Founder Asshole has called them in to work on a very important project that a month later will mean nothing to the Founder. Time and again, I have listened to Employees say that they were betting on what the future held. If they could just make it two more years, they would have all this money and a car, a house, their kids' braces, or their family vacations paid for in full.

I consistently push back with, "What is the price to your health, emotional well-being, and your family and friends watching you under this strain? How does it feel to numb yourself out until that magical day in the future? Is it really all worth it?" Working for a Founder is an amazing opportunity, and, yes, it can be bumpy, unpredictable, and sometimes unpleasant. Nevertheless, it is not about being an indentured servant. Working for a Founder Asshole is not about being a slave to incessant demands upon your life and soul.

At this point, you probably can tell how I feel about Founder Assholes. If you are working for a Founder Asshole, you do have options. So, what can you do when you find yourself in this situation? The answer has a direct correlation to self-awareness. The more you are aware of why you are there and what is motivating you to stay, the better you can navigate the situation.

- Ask yourself, "Why am I here?" Be clear and honest about why you are subjecting yourself to this environment and Founder.
- Set boundaries for what you will and will not tolerate. You can still control your self-esteem, self-confidence, and personal worth.
- Practice pushing back. It is not always easy. Even so, it will help you develop the strength of your voice. Here are a few examples: "I hear what you

are saying. At the same time, I don't appreciate you swearing at me as you say it." "I got your message, and I will take care of it. Going forward, can you please not attack me personally?" "I am happy to work here. I do need you to know, I want to be treated with respect." "It is completely unnecessary to make rude comments when we are discussing this topic."

👀 Know when enough is enough, and then find another career opportunity where you are celebrated for all you bring, and reconnect to joy in your work.

EMBRACE YOUR GENIUS

INSPIRING HEALTHY ENERGY JUICE

What tends to lift a Founder positively also lifts a team positively. Here are just a few actions that you can take to inspire Good Energy Juices without going to an extreme:

💡 Set up a brainstorming event, like "hackathons." Set a goal of innovating, solving, or creating something new—focus on the positive.

💡 Set up a "ten-years-from-now vision board" and ask everyone to post where they see the company in ten years. Revitalize the energy of the Founder and the team to shift the energy.

💡 Break free of your existing environment and ignite everyone's Creative Energy Juices. Go outside in nature, take a walk, volunteer, or just do something random in your community. Shake it up, shake it out, and shake it in some new directions.

💡 Find something to celebrate to bring everyone in and reconnect the Founder and the team as a reminder of why you are all in it together.

💡 If you really want to get the Good Energy Juices flowing, find a common enemy and create a shared vision to conquer it together. The enemy can be anything—a competitor, a social cause, a justice movement, or a goal that can be conquered.

Be inspired by the Founder you work with, not terrorized by a Founder Asshole. It is a choice that you, and only you, can make!

Love Your Journey

Stop

❌ Accepting poor and inappropriate Founder behaviors as part of your job

❌ Allowing yourself to be treated with disrespect or worse

❌ Idolizing the brilliance of your Founder Asshole

START

- ❯ Recognizing the different forms of the Founder's Energy Juice
- ❯ Supporting your Founder in a healthy and positive way
- ❯ Looking for a new job when you are finished with working for a Founder Asshole

WOODISM

"We are all people of value, no matter our titles, roles, positions, or bank accounts. Value yourself more than any opportunity or asshole."

The Roller Coaster of a Visionary Mind

SUCCESS PRACTICE 6

*Being an Employee in a Founder-led business
is very similar to riding a roller coaster.
There are twists and turns, ups and downs.
The key is strengthening your internal fortitude to
ride the ride and find joy in it at the same time.*

FOUNDEROLOGY REALITY

Working with Founders is much like a roller coaster ride. It can be a lot of fun even while you know there is always the chance of getting whiplash from the ride. Take this example of one Founder's roller coaster ride:

Week One—Fire Cassandra (Down Ride on the Roller Coaster)

Founder (to HR Manager): Please fire Cassandra.

HR: Why are we firing Cassandra?

Founder: I have repeatedly asked Cassandra to complete the weekly to-do list that I give her and let me know when she has achieved everything. She never finishes the entire list, and she never updates me on the list.

HR: Have you told Cassandra about her performance and how it needs to improve?

Founder: I tell her every week what she needs to get done and how I expect her to get it done.

HR: I will talk to Cassandra about her performance and how she can improve it.

Founder: Terrific. I will not assign Cassandra anything else to do, so I am less frustrated.

Week Two—Cassandra Getting New Projects (Sideways Ride on the Roller Coaster)

Cassandra: I was told by HR last week that I will not be getting any more projects.

Founder: Cassandra, that's true. You are not going to get any more projects like the ones you worked on previously. These are new projects.

Cassandra: HR told me not to work on any projects if I wanted to keep my job.

Founder: Cassandra, HR essentially works for me, and I will take care of it with them. Let's please focus on getting these projects done and not worry about HR.

Week Three—Cassie and HR (Sideways Ride on the Roller Coaster)

Founder: I just want you to know that Cassie is kicking ass and taking names. This is awesome.

HR: Who is Cassie? Did you hire someone new? Why wasn't I told about the new hire?

Founder: You know Cassie. She's worked here for over a year.

HR: I know no one named Cassie.

Founder: Well, that's why we have missed this superstar on the team. Honestly, please get out of your office and start meeting our team.

(HR later finds out that Cassie is Cassandra as the Founder has a habit of renaming Employees.)

Week Four—The Cassandra/Cassie Issue (Up Ride on the Roller Coaster)

Founder: Cassie, you are doing a great job. Please keep up the great work!

Cassandra: Thank you so much. I enjoy working on so many new projects.

Founder (to HR Manager): You need to get Cassie on the shortlist next time we talk about people for promotion.

HR: You mean Cassandra, the team member you wanted fired last month?

Founder: Who are you talking about? I am talking about Cassie.

HR: Cassie is Cassandra. You wanted her fired last month.

Founder: I didn't want her fired. You said we should fire her if she didn't improve. I for sure remember that conversation. And why am I calling her Cassie if her name is Cassandra? Why can't she just pick a name and stick with it? So, what is her real name?

"What the heck is going on with my HR Manager?" the Founder thinks as the HR Manager stomps away in frustration.

"OMG, Cassandra—Cassie?" the HR Manager thinks with every stomp they take as they walk away from the Founder.

FIND YOUR SANITY

Founders, just like everyone else, will have ups, downs, and all-arounds—it's just that theirs happen in a more public and influential manner.

Many Founders are both blessed and cursed with having visionary minds, minds that can see things no one else can see. Visionary minds have the power to see a picture of the future when others can only see pieces. A visionary mind is also an active mind, constantly thinking about the next step or steps for making a vision into a reality.

As a result, Founders and their businesses are inseparable. Ask a Founder how they are, and most will respond relative to how their businesses are doing, not how they are doing personally. Founders' emotions tend to mimic the ups and downs of their businesses, much like riding a roller coaster.

VISIONARY
MINDS
HAVE THE POWER
to see a picture of
THE FUTURE
when others can only
SEE PIECES.

What complicates this even further is that Founders tend to get taken off course by perceived amazing opportunities to accelerate or advance their visions. These amazing opportunities are sometimes referred to as shiny objects.

These shiny objects are here today because they are so shiny and the absolute best, and gone tomorrow because they are not really shiny. Shiny objects serve as amazing distractions when the roller coaster ride is not going well. Through the years, I have helped many Employees gain greater understanding into Founders' visionary minds by sharing insights of roller coasters and shiny objects.

THE FOUNDER'S ROLLER COASTER

The "Founder's Roller Coaster" is the term I developed to capture the essence of what all Founders know very well about the way their businesses move from incredible highs to difficult dips and sideways slides. It truly can feel like an unpredictable theme park ride.

However, for most Founders, growing their businesses and moving it upward and forward brings about many behaviors, feelings, and emotions that don't always move up. Being able to read where a Founder is on the roller coaster is a key skill for understanding how you can contribute and thrive while helping to minimize the impact of the extreme highs and lows of the roller coaster ride.

Here are the general behaviors of a Founder on a roller coaster, depending on which direction the company is headed at any particular moment.

FOUNDER	"UP" Behaviors	"DOWN" Behaviors	"SIDEWAYS" Behaviors
Action	Celebration days, visible and joyous	Frustration days, withdrawn and quiet	Combo good and bad days, unpredictable
Emotions	Feel euphoric	Feel anger and frustration	Energy is up and down
Feelings	All positive feelings about the team	Feel that everyone needs to be fired	Lots of different directions for the team
Leadership	Generous with their time and money	Take control of everything, especially money	Control is situational and unexpected
Decision-Making	Make decisions with ease	Stop making decisions; everything is stalled	Make random decisions based on feelings
Employee	Enjoy the ride	Manage through this part of the ride	Help push the ride forward

THE "UP" RIDE

Riding the roller coaster up is one of the most exhilarating and fun times of working with a Founder. This is when everything in the entire company is firing on all cylinders. Business is good, projects are being completed on time and correctly, and the working environment is joyful, exciting, and some days feels like a party, and in fact turns into parties. The Founder's generosity is overflowing. Employees are getting rewards, prizes, trips, and every day new buffets of food and drinks are showing up at work. If the business is winning, then everyone is winning—it's an amazing experience. Most Founders can ride the roller coaster most comfortably when the direction is up.

The up part of the ride is awesome, and it is at this point of the ride I encourage everyone to enjoy the ride. You are working hard, you are giving it your best, and you deserve the recognition and rewards of all your efforts. I also advise Employees to take this moment to really enjoy their Founder and see the very best of their hearts, spirits, and their true care for the entire team. These are great times for everyone.

THE "DOWN" RIDE

The down ride of the roller coaster is the exact opposite of the up part of the ride. Think about it in real life when you are on an actual roller coaster. Going up is fun. You can see the entire park; you can chat with your friend sitting next to you; and the ride is very much in control. Once you get to the top, things change quickly, and in a matter of seconds, you go from enjoying the view to holding on for dear life as you are hurtling toward the ground at lightning speed. What once was so enjoyable has now become a terror ride. The only difference is, on a ride, you know when the drop is coming. With a Founder, you do not know when a Founder is about to start hurtling downward. The good news is there are ways to be aware the ride is shifting down.

There are many triggers that can shift a Founder into the down part of their ride. Here are some of the triggers you can look for to anticipate your ride starting to go down. They range from the Founder feeling a loss of control, starting meetings with concerns that the company is falling behind (though there is no evidence), a perceived attack by new competition, being angry over monthly financial statements even when they are positive, or verbalizing that people are not working hard enough.

And sometimes it can be as simple as one Employee telling the Founder, "This is a nice chance to get a break from our highly driven intensity for a change and be able to celebrate our success." That simple statement can shift the up to the down in a matter of minutes. We have all seen it happen.

Whatever the trigger is, the response is generally the same. Everyone needs to get back to work—working harder, producing bigger and better results. The highly driven Founder is now in hyperdrive. The Founder will continue to express their unhappiness with everyone and everything until new and better results are achieved.

The down part of the ride is not easy, and, in many cases, it whiplashes the Employees. The whiplash can look like this: yesterday we were eating free pizza and laughing at lunch, and today we all need to sit at our desks and eat in silence. And the one Employee that did not get the "memo" that the down part of the ride has happened will be written up for not taking their job and business situation seriously the minute they return from their lunch.

THE "SIDEWAYS" RIDES

Perhaps the most difficult stage for a Founder, as well as the team, is the sideways stage. Sideways is tough. It is the equivalent of running in place, super hard, and going nowhere. It's referred to as "being stuck in the suck." This is where a Founder must tap into their superhuman strength to rally. This can be with a new vision, a new competitive enemy, or a new cause—whatever is necessary to get the business back on track. Believe it or not, this is one of a Founder's greatest strengths: digging deep and rallying the business when it is stuck in the suck of sideways.

For example, let's say a Founder's business burns to the ground. As many stand around crying about the loss of the business, stuck in the loss, the Founder takes a moment, stands in the ashes, and, like a phoenix, rises and declares, "We will rebuild bigger and better. We will do it as a team, for our success, our customers, ourselves, our communities, and for the generations of people to come. Let these ashes serve as our fuel to recommit, to rebuild. This is no longer *my* business; it is *our* business."

This is one of many Founders' secret talents in action—rallying everyone to a new vision. Even when everything and everyone says it is impossible, Founders will make it happen.

EMBRACE YOUR GENIUS

RIDING THE ROLLER COASTER

Many Employees want consistency, predictability, and routine in their workplace. I think this is possible in a static and mature organization. A Founder-led business is dynamic and ever-changing. What is predictable is that no two days will ever be the same with a Founder. It does not mean it is always chaotic and disorganized. Yet, it is sometimes messy, this is true. It means more often than not, the business will always be moving up, down, and sideways, just like a roller coaster.

There are many opportunities to stay on track when riding the Founder's roller coaster. You can best support a Founder and keep your own sanity if you learn the signs of the ride.

Start with a quick read of the situation to determine whether the Founder is up, down, or sideways. Once you know where the Founder is, adjust to the Founder's current state. Enjoy the ups, recognize the downs, and find agility in the sideways. Employees who seize the opportunity to identify and even anticipate the ride signs develop greater abilities to be less affected by the roller coaster, both personally and professionally.

You can also increase your ability to better see the signs by learning the specific differences between how a Founder behaves and what a Founder says in each stage of the ride. Here is a classic example: a Founder is speaking at an all-team meeting, telling everyone that the company is in financial hardship and that there are no funds available for anything extra. The Founder paints a bleak doomsday scenario. At the conclusion of the meeting, the Founder lets everyone know they are leaving for a three-week vacation and will be unavailable during their time away.

I hear from Employees all the time, "WTF was that all about? Are we really failing? Are we going to lose our jobs? Why are they going on vacation if we are going broke?" With mixed messages like this, look for facts, and assess your situation with facts and figures versus rhetoric and rumors. The facts could be the business is doing great, and the Founder just wanted to fire everyone up prior to leaving on vacation.

Your opportunity is to gain and keep real-time awareness of the current situation, gauge the reality of the situation, and stay focused on your work and making an impact. Your best way to grow with the company is to remember to control what you can control and not be overly distracted by the roller coaster. Your absolute best opportunities come when you enjoy the highs, keep steady sideways, and realize that the downs are just moments in time, not for all time.

SHINY OBJECT SYNDROME

Founders are amazing at creating, finding, and chasing shiny objects. Shiny objects are anything that attracts a Founder's eye, and the Founder is compelled to look because they are shiny and new. Shiny objects allow a Founder to remain in a perpetual state of starting something new. Shiny objects syndrome is especially prevalent when a Founder is on the downside of the roller coaster. Shiny objects syndrome sometimes serves as an escape vehicle from the pressures of the moment.

When acted upon, a shiny object not only demands a Founder's attention and focus; it can also pull you and the entire company out of alignment. A shiny object can be a random idea, initiative, or project that came out of nowhere and superficially makes no sense. Founders are insatiable shiny-object-idea chasers—especially when the ideas can be rationalized as research, business expansion, brand extension, or any type of improvement.

Shiny objects, left unchecked, can become distractions and delay business growth. When leveraged, though, shiny objects can sometimes serve as opportunities for product innovation, new service lines, and brilliant ideas for growth that just need to be implemented at a different point in time. The key is for you to see the value in a shiny object without getting completely distracted by them.

EMBRACE YOUR GENIUS

NAVIGATING SHINY OBJECT SYNDROME

These pro tips will support you in navigating shiny objects syndrome. Pro-tip number one: never say no to a Founder's shiny objects. Just say yes. Telling Founders, "No," is the same as asking them to "double down and go for it." When shiny objects appear, go back to a technique previously mentioned about asking clarifying questions and now add one more question. Ask the following three questions:

- 💡 What are the specific deliverables for the ask, request, or assignment?
- 💡 What is the timeframe for the deliverable?
- 💡 Are *you* okay with delaying another initiative to address this opportunity?

Most Employees misunderstand the fleeting significance of a shiny object and immediately engage in the Founder's fire drill and stop doing their current work and start chasing the shiny objects too.

Unfortunately, when Employees start chasing the shiny objects, a whole lot of extra work, effort, and drama are created for everyone. All this can be quickly mitigated if the Employee simply says yes to the Founder. Saying yes does not mean running the fire drill to make it happen; it simply is the acknowledgment of the shiny object. Life becomes much easier when you agree the shiny objects are indeed cool, instead of trying to explain the million reasons why it will never work. Employees who use the three questions for clarity find that shiny objects will disappear more quickly too.

Pro-tip number two for thriving: as mentioned earlier with the three questions, remember that most Founders are verbal processors, so when they are throwing out shiny objects, understand they're doing this to make sure these flashes of brilliance are not lost.

I always suggest to Employees to utilize visible displays of listening. Said differently, show the Founder you have heard them by finding a visible home for the shiny objects. You can find shiny objects a home on a flipchart, a spreadsheet, in any kind of app, shared files, or on a planning document. This technique of documenting the idea and capturing it validates you heard and respected the Founder. It is the perfect way to find a "yes" without having to give the Founder a "no."

One truly never knows when a shiny object will become a brilliant business idea and change the world.

LOVE YOUR JOURNEY

STOP

- ✖ Thinking every day is going to be the same
- ✖ Being dismissive of shiny objects, publicly and privately
- ✖ Rehashing a history of shiny objects that did not work in the past

START

- ❯ Learning the signs of the roller coaster
- ❯ Enjoying the up of the ride and managing through the down and sideways
- ❯ Finding a yes in every no with shiny objects

WOODISM

"You don't know until you try—find a yes in every no."

*An Employee who isn't moving the company
forward is holding it back from its future.*

FOUNDEROLOGY REALITY

*Here is a re-enactment of so many Founder conversations
through the years:*

Founder: How can we keep him?

Kathleen: We can't. He has had numerous roles in the
company, and the performance is always the
same—nonexistent.

Founder: What else can we do so that he can stay?

Kathleen: We have tried everything—performance plans,
development plans, sending him to seminars,
giving him an accountability partner, demoting
him, and cutting him out of the team.

Founder: I hate this. Is there anything else I can do?

Kathleen: You can pay him personally to be your assistant.

Founder: I don't want to pay him personally, and I don't
think he is capable of being my assistant.

Kathleen: Okay, he can stay if you are good with higher overhead, supporting a noncontributing Employee, and continuing to accept the drama of it all.

Founder: Look, we have got to find a way. He has been with me since the beginning.

Kathleen: I get it. There is nothing worse than this moment. However, if you are going to grow your company, you need to have Employees who can grow with it.

A discussion like this one can go back and forth for days and sometimes weeks or months. It once took almost two years for the Founder to decide if one Employee needed to leave the company. I don't know if the Founder decided because they knew it was time or if all the conversations just wore down the Founder to make a decision.

When the Employee was finally let go, the Founder said, "Wow, what was I waiting for? Things have immediately improved." I wanted to jump up and down with joy. The enormous amount of time and energy we had put into talking about this one Employee holding back the company was finally over!

These conversations with the Founder are about individuals I call Cultural Candles. These non-contributors are typically a Founder's loyal, trusted friend or a family member a Founder just can't let go.

FIND YOUR SANITY

Letting a Cultural Candle go is the absolute hardest, most gut-wrenching, most difficult decision a Founder will ever make. It has very little to do with business. It is all personal/emotional, and there is no way to rationalize it. Only Founders can make this decision, and they always make it on their own timeline—no matter what the consequences are to the business, the team, and themselves. Many Founders would rather lose their businesses, great Employees, and potential growth of their businesses than blow out their Cultural Candle.

I could write another entire book on Founders, Employees, Cultural Candles, and their impact on business performance. Employees are the most valuable asset in any business. They are the heart, soul, and hands who transform the Founder's vision into reality.

In Founder-led businesses, there are two areas relative to the team I spend a considerable amount of effort on to support a company in its growth. One area is maximizing team performance, and the other is on the impact of Cultural Candles. Both areas are key components for optimizing Employee and business performance. They both play a critical role in a Founder-led business. Understanding these dynamics will support your long-term success.

THE DYNAMICS OF TEAM PERFORMANCE

Founders have this belief that better Employees—better hires—get better results. No one can really fault that logic. Consequently, Founders make having the very best team one of their number-one priorities. This commitment should be music to the ears of Employees and those tasked with finding top talent.

There is a disparity that exists between a Founder's performance expectations and human resource performance expectations as it relates to top talent. This disparity can cause frustration on all sides. Look at the difference in performance expectations.

Founder versus HR Performance Perspectives	
Founder	**HR**
"I hire people who immediately know their jobs."	"People need time to learn."
"Everyone should anticipate what I need."	"People cannot read minds."
"No one moves fast enough."	"People are moving fast; they have only been here a week."
"No one moves fast enough."	"People are moving fast; they have only been here a week."
"How many times do I need to explain things?"	"Please explain more than once."
"Why can't we just find great people?"	"Great people are here— they are just uninformed."
"I want loyal people who will be here forever."	"People need a reason to commit."

However, the universal pursuit of exceptional, brilliant, lifelong Employees who pledge unwavering loyalty to the company is where the Founder gets trapped—between their performance expectations and everyone else's reality of performance. Of course, all Founders would love their Employees to dedicate their lives to the company. Yet, the constant pressure to find these rare lifelong Employees becomes a Founder's point of frustration.

Some Founders can become so obsessed with this search that they completely miss the amazing performance of their current Employees, like you. All of this only continues to perpetuate the Founder's need for finding more and better loyal Employees.

Founders tend to believe no one is committed to their business as much as they are—which, of course, is true. It can be very frustrating for Employees to know that a Founder may never be satisfied no matter how amazing their work ethic, contributions, and impact are in the business.

My advice to Employees is always to understand it is not personal, even though at times it can feel very personal. It truly is about the Founder pushing to find those super committed and lifelong, loyal Employees willing to do whatever it takes. Unfortunately, it is just not realistic to expect every Employee to have all these qualities. Founders with these expectations find themselves in a spin cycle of never-ending complaining/worrying about the lack of talent in their business.

Embrace Your Genius

Amplifying Your Performance

There are several areas of opportunity for you with a Founder who is caught in a continuous spin cycle. Perspective is a key point to keep in mind—there is a saying: "Your perception is your reality." Look at the gaps again in performance expectations between a Founder and human resources.

One of the greatest opportunities often underutilized by Employees is to amplify their accomplishments, achievements, or contributions for the Founder to see and hear. This is not typical Employee behavior in most organizations. It is an important one for you to learn in a Founderled organization. It is key for you to share your accomplishments and contributions because this raises your Founder's awareness and consciousness of the real impact you are making in their business.

Shining a light on your contributions is an amazing opportunity to share successes and results in a positive way. It is an equally critical activity to support Founders in keeping a realistic perspective about your amazing efforts and impact on their business. It also very effectively slows down the Founder's spin cycle!

The question is how you can share your accomplishments and not look like you are showing off or being disrespectful? My answer is simple; it is all about raising awareness through raising your voice or your hand and making your Founder aware. I have heard so many Employees say things like, "They should know—why should I tell them—this is stupid." Say whatever you want. However, most Founders have so much on their proverbial plate they don't know everything. Here are a few great ways you can raise awareness:

- Start each meeting sharing a success story/ achievement.
- Develop scorecards for success, measure what is meaningful, and consistently share the results with the Founder and Employees.
- Introduce celebrations of meaningful achievements and ensure the Founder is present for the celebrations.
- Use creative visual displays, such as posters, charts, and graphs of accomplishments.
- Incorporate random acts of success acknowledgments for Employees who go above and beyond.

CULTURAL CANDLES IMPACT

The spin cycle of team performance is further complicated by Cultural Candles. Unfortunately, as the Founder tries to grow the business, the Founder continues to accommodate these mismatched Cultural Candles with new titles and reduced responsibilities instead of letting them go. Cultural Candles are not defined by their length of time at the company; they are really defined by their loyal relationship with the Founder.

Cultural Candles are revered by most Founders and vilified by most productive Employees. Why? Because who do you think picks up the slack of the Cultural Candles? That's right, you! Cultural Candles are very real blind spots for Founders; they simply do not see the incompetence of the loyal Cultural Candles. Or, if a Founder does see the incompetence, they will deny it or shift the blame to something or someone else. There are many pain points for Founders trying to grow their businesses, but none hold a candle (pun intended) to blowing out the Cultural Candles of the company.

Employees simply cannot understand what hold the Cultural Candle has over the Founder. Incriminating photographs? Stories of skeletons in the closet? The hold is a strong emotional connection. As the opening *Founderology* Reality illustrates, Cultural Candles simply cannot just be ex-tinguished.

GETTING BURNED BY A CULTURAL CANDLE

Even the best Employees can get burned by a Cultural Candle. Being a Founder can be very lonely, so when there is a Cultural Candle to provide unconditional support, a Founder is indebted with gratitude. There is an impenetrable bond between a Founder and Cultural

Candle. The bond is forged through the Founder's vulnerability or other powerful emotional connections. Coming between this bond is usually where Employees stumble. You must realize that when you complain about or disparage a Cultural Candle, you are simultaneously saying the same thing about your Founder. Many Employees have had their careers singed or put out by not truly understanding the depth and power of this very important bond.

CULTURAL CANDLES AND BUSINESS GROWTH

In over twenty years of working with many Founders, I have experienced the greatest moments of truth in our working relationships when we had honest conversations about Cultural Candles. In its purest essence, the conversation is not about the Cultural Candle or me. It is a moment of truth for the Founder.

It really forces the Founder to address the questions, "Am I really ready to transform my business from where we are to where I really want it to go? Am I ready to move from okay to good to great?" How the Founder answers those questions and acts upon them determines the next steps in terms of who is staying, who is going, and how the business is going to grow.

I can also honestly say that, as a Founder myself, I have created and enabled a few Cultural Candles, too. Sadly, there is nothing more frustrating for a Founder than realizing the person they have done so much for, given so much to, and truly taken along on the journey, in good times and bad, is a Cultural Candle—and they must be blown out.

EMBRACE YOUR GENIUS

DIMMING CULTURAL CANDLES

The absolute best and most insightful advice I can provide you regarding Cultural Candles is to know this is not a war you will ultimately win even if you think you are right. Even if you have proof that you are right, you will not win. You may win small battles. Trust me: you will ultimately lose the war. Cultural Candles are and will be forever only something a Founder can blow out.

There are several things you can do to **dim** a Cultural Candle, and the following are my go-to moves for dealing with them:

- 💡 Stay consistent in your performance and results. The more consistent you are, the more erratic and inconsistent a Cultural Candle appears. Believe me, it happens every time!
- 💡 Keep your composure, no matter how right or wrong you feel about a Cultural Candle. Accept that they are a fixture in your business until the Founder lets them go. Blowing up, publicly getting upset, or having outbursts does not serve a purpose. Yes, I understand that it is frustrating.

However, when you blow up, you look erratic, and the Cultural Candle looks just fine—again!

💡 Keep focused on your job and responsibilities. However, do not be the "fall guy" for Cultural Candles. There is no need to mask their lack of contribution, no need to do their work for the team, and no need to not say anything if asked specific questions about who did what on a project or assignment.

💡 Avoid openly challenging the Founder in any public setting relative to a Cultural Candle, even if everyone tells you to do it. This is a guaranteed kiss-of-death move for your career.

💡 Don't accept or tolerate any inappropriate behaviors or language from a Cultural Candle. Sometimes, Cultural Candles are the worst violators of company policy and procedures. Report inappropriate behaviors to someone in authority other than the Founder.

Remember, don't let a Cultural Candle steal your light. You always have the power to shine your light on your contributions, commitment, and performance, so your Founder sees what an exceptional Employee you are in growing their business.

Love Your Journey

Stop

- ❌ Complaining about Cultural Candles (it keeps them burning longer)
- ❌ Publicly battling with Cultural Candles
- ❌ Trying to accommodate Cultural Candles

Start

- ❯ Raising your voice and your hands to create awareness of your impact
- ❯ Shining your own light on your contributions and results
- ❯ Developing visual displays of accomplishments and achievements

WOODISM

"What you focus on grows. If a person is not moving us forward, they are holding us back from our future. Growing a company requires bright lights, not candles."

Driving For Growth

The more control you let go of, the more control you get.

FOUNDEROLOGY REALITY
INTERNAL CONFLICT CONVERSATIONS

Founders inevitably have numerous internal conflict conversations about growth and their desire to grow. Here are some great examples of Founder internal conflict conversations:

"I want the business to grow, AND I ...
>   ... don't want to let go of control."
>   ... want every decision to go through me."
>   ... need a team I can really trust."
>   ... know there are no good people out there."
>   ... am tired and exhausted."
>   ... don't want to deal with any more risk."

The Employees think, WTF is going on with my Founder? Some days, the business moves at a hundred miles per hour, while other days, the business is at an absolute standstill. Still other days, Employees are waiting for the next set of directions. Are they growing or staying? Who knows how the business will grow?!

FIND YOUR SANITY

A Founder continually struggles with this internal conflict; every waking thought is consumed by whether the business should stay in its current place or grow. They often keep these deeply personal conversations to themselves and rarely express such conflict out loud.

Believe me, these conversations are always happening. In fact, they happen around the clock for Founders. Even if they never open up about these internal conflict conversations, the impact of these internal conversations typically shows up in a Founder's actions. This can often seem very confusing and puts added pressure on Employees to figure out what is going on with the growth of the company.

For example, take a Founder who has been very successful initially with their business and in discussions about growing. Everyone is excited and, to a certain extent, so is the Founder. Except that growing the business is also connected to the Founder's need for control, and the Founder is not excited about letting go of more control. As we know, control is another part of a Founder's DNA.

The other less obvious issue is when a Founder reaches a certain level of success, their appetite for risk may change. When Founders move from survival mode to having steady and substantial cash in the bank, do they suddenly want to risk it? They have been risking it since the beginning. Can't they just enjoy it? As a result, control starts to shift toward "hanging on to what we have" versus "growing/risking more."

Again, how a Founder behaves is the more accurate indicator of their commitment to growth versus what a Founder says. Founders can say all day long that they want to grow. However, if their behaviors are not moving in any direction to support actions toward growth, they are literally showing you their inner conflict.

Understanding the impact of these internal-conflict conversations in Founders in both their words and their actions will give you incredible insights into what is happening relative to the growth of the company.

THREE PATHS TO GROWTH

How does a Founder of a $100 million company or a $50,000 business—whatever the size, it doesn't matter—squelch their inner conflict and grow? Many business pundits will say there are unlimited ways to grow a business. I would completely agree.

There are many ways to grow, but as it relates specifically to Founders, there are three primary paths to growth:
1. The Founder leaves.
2. The Founder keeps control.
3. The Founder leads through the team.

Path One: The Founder Leaves

One path every Founder has available is to sell the company and leave. This might sound extreme, yet it is very commonplace in business. The reason for this is that there are various kinds of Founders. I categorize them as:

CREATORS
Those who create original concepts, get them up and running, and then sell them.

BUILDERS
those who take a concept, build it for future growth, and then sell it.

GROWERS
Those who scale a concept for long-term growth before eventually selling it.

Founders can generally lean into at least one of these categories. Understanding the predominant driver of your Founder will assist you in gaining greater insights into what drives their position to stay, leave, or grow their business. You can tell what type of Founder you work for by recognizing these Founder behaviors in the lifecycle of the business.

Founder Growth Profiles

FOUNDER PROFILE	DRIVER	CONFLICT	BEHAVIORS
Creator ("Ideator")	Creates a concept and gets it up and running	No one will ever understand my thought process for what makes this so special	Always tries new things; starts many projects but finishes few; high abandonment of ideas
Builder	Takes an existing concept, builds and leads it, and may or may not grow it	No one will ever know how to lead or manage this without simplifying it or making it ordinary for the masses	Invests time in developing and implementing order, structure, systems, and planning; these exist to get things done to ensure everything is done the Founder's way
Grower	Grows and scales a concept in the short- or long-term	There is a high probability that my concept will become mediocre if left to people who don't know it	Looks to grow and scale a concept to have a significant place in the market while still maintaining control

Whether Founders get their drive from creating, building, or growing, there is a high probability they will look to depart when they have exhausted all their creative outlets. There is no right or wrong to this reality, and there is also no need for judgment. It really comes down to this: is the Founder still creatively challenged and doing what they love? Just like most things in life, when the love is gone, typically so is the relationship.

When a Founder is contemplating leaving, it starts to look and sound like this:

"I need to take two hours off."
"I need to take half a day off."
"I need to take a day off."
"I need to take two days off."
"I need to take a weekend off."
"I need to take a week off."
"I need to take two weeks off."
"I need to take a month off."
"I need to take a sabbatical."
"Bottom line, I need to get out."

Or it can be acted out: "I'm going to wrap up all of this and sell this damned business. Then I won't have to deal with it anymore. I am done."

Ultimately, in cases where Founders leave, they are stepping out, either incrementally or with just one big step. They truly believe their only option is to opt-out and leave if they are going to save themselves and their businesses.

EMBRACE YOUR GENIUS

YOUR OPPORTUNITY WHEN THE FOUNDER LEAVES

You can still succeed when a Founder leaves with these three great moves:

- You can support a Founder in their transition by being a resource of intellectual capital and knowledge for both the Founder and the team in the transition.
- You can be an advocate for a positive change for the Founder and the Employee team.
- You can also recognize how you can support the new management team in a transition.

Path Two: The Founder Controls

A Founder-centric business is one where *everything* must go through the Founder. This is everything from big strategic decisions to buying paperclips. At the core of a Founder-centric business is the Founder's relationship with control.

There are two major control factors. The first is the Founder's need to have complete control. The second is the Founder's fear of losing control. Either way, the result is the same—a Founder-centric business is born when every decision, strategy, and thought must be run by the Founder before anything is done or executed.

A Founder-centric business inadvertently develops a team of followers instead of a team of leaders. As the company grows, the Founder unintentionally builds legions of followers. As the business grows, more followers are added. The followers all learn how to not do anything independent of the Founder or suffer the consequences.

This results in increasing the grind on the Founder to lead never-ending day-to-day details and make all decisions.

Without some type of leadership or mindset shift, most Founders become fatigued by the incessant grind. This is when the Founder starts to contemplate leaving because they see the way their business is operating only through them, and they can't figure how to grow or change direction. They have no leaders, and no one has been developed to lead. Many Founders, tired and exhausted, make the decision to leave.

Although it would appear easier to have every decision made by a single person like a Founder, it is not a sustainable or scalable business model for growth. It may work in small companies and dictatorships, but it does not work for growing businesses.

Embrace Your Genius

Your Opportunity in a Founder-Centric Control

There are two key mindsets that enable you to win in a Founder-centric business:

First, accept how a Founder-centric business operates. You can gain invaluable experience in learning how to navigate it. Remember, you can still control a great deal even in a Founder-centric environment. This includes your attitude, performance, contributions, and voice. You may not be the final decision maker. You can be a decision influencer or a voice in the right direction.

Second, learn to recognize the signs of what Founders are looking for when they make decisions. Begin aligning your work and results to the rhythm of how the Founder makes their decisions.

The following is a classic illustration of something most Employees would perceive as not being mission critical. Yet, in this example, you will be able to see how you can learn a Founder's rhythm for making decisions. Let's say your Founder is looking for a new T-shirt design. For most Employees, it is a T-shirt, but for a Founder, the T-shirt represents the brand, the look, the logo and will serve to create a legion of walking billboards. That's why, for the Founder, the process always has so many more steps other than "just picking a T-shirt."

The T-Shirt design process will illustrate the Founder's decision rhythm:

- The Employee is asked to provide the entire *universe of T-shirt types (rhythm),* T-shirt designs, T-Shirt fabrics, and T-shirt ideas.
- The Founder selects *three to five options* (rhythm) from the entire universe.
- The Employee continues to work with the Founder through multiple rounds, and I mean *multiple rounds* (rhythm) of revisions until there are one or two options left.

- 💡 The Founder sees these rounds of revision as *collaboration* (rhythm). The Employee sees it as never-ending. The multiple revisions continue until one option is ultimately selected.
- 💡 The Employee is elated the T-Shirt is done. The Founder now starts a *new revision process to perfect* (rhythm) the final T-Shirt version. The revisions continue until the Founder is 100 percent satisfied.
- 💡 The T-Shirt is completed. *The Founder is ecstatic* (rhythm); the Employee is exhausted.

Your opportunity as an Employee is to learn the rhythm from the experience and not be exhausted by it. Take the key learnings and apply them going forward on projects for the Founder. If this is your Founder's rhythm, don't be frustrated by it; embrace it as their decision-making process.

When you learn the rhythm of the Founder's decision-making process, you will see just how much it applies in almost everything a Founder does. When you have mastered the Founder's rhythm, you have what I call **liquid gold**—*Founder and Employee Alignment.*

Once you have mastered this decision-making rhythm, it will save you hours and days of frustration. As the saying goes, the more you know, the more you grow.

Take the
KEY LEARNINGS
AND APPLY THEM
GOING

FORWARD
on projects for the Founder.

Path Three: Founder Leads

In a Founder-led organization, *led* is the key word. The business has a clear direction and a plan, which is directed by the Founder. The Founder is still in control of their business. Now they are operating from a leadership position versus the *doer*ship position that exists in a Founder-centric business.

How does a Founder make the transition from *doer*ship— or doing and deciding everything—to *leader*ship and to ultimately leading the business? The simplest yet most complex answer is this: the Founder *must* embrace their own leadership transformation. One of my leadership mantras I share with Founders is this one —*the more control you let go of, the more control you get.*

What prevents most Founders from making the leadership transformation is again simple: *something related to fear.* Fear stops the Founder from letting go. There are no other answers. There are others that come up like trust, being burned, trying it before and failing, etc., but in truth, they all lead back to one and one place only—*fear.*

Founders can successfully let go when they realize the difference between abdication and delegation. Abdication is assigning a person to lead with no plan, system, structures, communication tools, or resources.

An everyday example of abdication is when the Founder literally turns over responsibility to an Employee, even though the Employee is not set up or properly prepared for success in any form or fashion. The Employee does their best operating in the dark, working very hard, yet still does not meet the Founder's expectations. The Founder has another conversation with the Employee to reset the expectations. The Employee, not wanting to let the Founder down, acknowledges their understanding even though maybe not truly understanding. The Employee again works hard yet misses the mark on the Founder's expectations once again. Now, the Founder is even more disappointed and growing more upset by each reset.

The Founder continues to let go of control, and the Employee still can't make it happen. Thus, leading the Founder to their self-fulfilling prophecy that no one can do what they do. The Founder then rationalizes why their initial hesitancy in not wanting to let go of control proves to be true too.

Delegation is about a Founder preparing others for success. When Founders delegate responsibility with a clear vision, mission, plan of action, and accountability, they exponentially increase their potential for success. Will the Employee stumble, struggle, and have moments of failure along the way? Of course, they will. They are human and with time, patience, coaching, and feedback, the Employee *will* succeed.

This is a hypothetical story I often share with Founders and Employees to make my point about the importance of delegation. Two teams are at the edge of a forest on a cold and dark night, and they must get to the other side of the forest to save their lives. One team is led by a person with a clear vision, mission, and plan to get to the other side quickly and efficiently. The other is led by a person who is completely underprepared and barking out orders in every direction. They have no vision, no mission, and no plan.

Who would you rather follow?

Now, whenever I have this "leadership transformation" conversation with Founders, I ask this very funny question: "Why do you have all these people working here if none of them work?"

Founders typically reply: "I ask myself that same question. It's crazy."

Then I push further: "So, why keep them—the overhead, the expense?"

Founders usually reply, "Well, someone has to do the work. Somehow, all the Employees who are here are doers, waiting to be told what to do next. What I really need are more leaders."

This is the moment the Founder has their personal moment of truth, and the discussion of transforming from *doer*ship to leadership begins. The Founder realizes the potential of significant growth in *leader*ship and performance when letting go of control comes through delegation and not abdication.

EMBRACE YOUR GENIUS

BUILDING FOUNDER CONFIDENCE IN YOU!

The more confidence a Founder has in you, the more control the Founder will give you. Here are three things you can do right now to build even more confidence with your Founder. First, like it has been previously mentioned, always seek clarity on the assignment, even if the Founder is super busy; they will always have time for you—so ask for time and seek clarity.

Second, Founders hate surprises! If you are going to miss a deadline, date, or deliverable, be proactive. No matter how chill, easy-going, or nice your Founder is—Founders still don't like surprises. Finally, the day you "think" you can read the Founder's mind and don't need to ask for specifics anymore is also the day the Founder takes back their control. Building Founder confidence is an ongoing practice that can produce terrific opportunities for you.

The opportunity to excel is exactly why you took the job, to be a part of growing a great brand with a brilliant Founder. Give your Founder every reason to have confidence in your voice, actions, and leadership. This is the ultimate opportunity to go for it and win!

LOVE YOUR JOURNEY

STOP

- ✗ Protecting Founders from themselves (they don't need your protection)
- ✗ Complaining about why you can't do more if you are not taking care of what you have responsibility for now
- ✗ Worrying about the Founder's future and focus on being your best today

START

- ❯ Realizing how much Founders have "let go to you" and take care of it
- ❯ Finding your Founder's rhythm for making decisions and align to it
- ❯ Letting your words, actions, and performance serve to build confidence with your Founder

WOODISM

"Control what you can control and let go of the rest."

The Extraordinary Gap

SUCCESS PRACTICE 9

"Fail Forward Magnificently."
This is a core value of Suzy's Swirl,
my family-owned business.
Translation: I would rather go down swinging big
than by standing there holding a bat.

FOUNDEROLOGY REALITY

The Extraordinary Gap is the space where a vision of something epically amazing collides with the everyday ordinary. The following are scenarios of how an Extraordinary Gap manifests itself in a Founder-led business:

SCENARIO 1

The Founder has a vision for how everyone will be amazed by the incredible entertainment at the next company holiday party. The Founder spends months before the party finding the absolute perfect band. The Founder spares no expense of time or resources. In the Founder's mind, everyone will be blown away and tell everyone they know it was the best company holiday party they ever attended.

REALITY

The Employees arrive at the party and enjoy the entertainment. They think it is good background music for the event. The Employees really enjoy seeing each other and catching up outside of the workplace.

EXTRAORDINARY GAP

Founder— "This was a once-in-a-lifetime event."
Employee— "Thanks, the food and music were great."

Scenario 2

The Founder has a vision for Employee orientation and how, at the conclusion of the orientation, all new Employees will pledge their allegiance and loyalty to the company because they will be so impressed by the company.

REALITY

The orientation is exciting for the Employees, and at the end, each Employee is required to sign a document for human resources acknowledging they understand the policies of the company.

EXTRAORDINARY GAP

Founder— "Every Employee will be inspired and love our company."
Employee— "I am excited to work here. It seems like a great company. Now I need to go finish my paperwork."

Scenario 3

The Founder has an exact vision for the development and execution of the company's training program.

REALITY

The first thing the Founder hears from the Employee is that there is a lot of writing required in the program.

EXTRAORDINARY GAP

Founder— "World-class, life-changing company training program."
Employee— "It's a lot of work."

Scenario 4

The Founder has a vision that each customer experience should be filled with joy. They see every customer leaving their business in a state of happiness from their experience and then telling everyone they know about it.

REALITY

The Founder stops visiting their store because it infuriates them to see the customer service level, which is not close to the expected vision, and worse, the customer thinks the experience is just okay.

EXTRAORDINARY GAP

Founder— "A revolutionized way of providing a customer experience."
Customer— "It's an okay customer experience."

FIND YOUR SANITY

Founders are inspired and motivated to take the impossible and make it possible. Unfortunately, a Founder's vision of extraordinary is often met with the reality that making the impossible possible is not as easy as they might think. The Extraordinary Gap is the space where a vision of something epically amazing collides with the everyday ordinary.

The Extraordinary Gap's size directly correlates to how demoralized and potentially depressed the Founder will become based on the gap. At times, the Extraordinary Gap can be small and unnoticeable, while other times, it can be as wide as the Grand Canyon. The Extraordinary Gap almost always slows or stops the forward momentum of Employees or the business.

THE POWER OF THE EXTRAORDINARY GAP

Founders usually can recover from their disappointment over events not going as amazingly as they initially envisioned for such things as company holiday parties, meetings, and other company-related social activities. When it comes to their ideas for moving their business forward, there is much less room for tolerating the gap. Understanding the difference between a Founder's views of the Extraordinary Gap versus an Employee's interpretation can be an eye-opening experience. Take a moment and think about your perspective and approach to closing the gap with your Founder.

Founder Perspective	Employee Perspective
"This is not my vision."	"It's close to what you said."
"Why did we change this?"	"It's better for everyone to do it this way."
"Why aren't these up to my standards?"	"They are—we only made changes to make it easier for everyone."
"Why does it look like this?"	"What's wrong with it?"
"I am tired of repeating myself all the time."	"I don't see why this is such a big deal."

Most Employees underestimate the size of the Extraordinary Gap. The reason for this is that most Employees accept what a Founder says and believe this is their actual opinion. If the Founder says the result is okay, most Employees take that answer at face value and think, "It's truly not that big of a deal."

This approach is one of the single biggest mistakes you can make with a Founder. What Employees miss is that the Founder takes that "not that big of a deal" statement as a mortal wound. Big and small gaps for Founders are merely more examples of their vision falling into the dull and ordinary. The one place no highly driven Founder ever wants their vision to land is at ordinary.

Even with the Extraordinary Gap, it does not stop the Founder from trying again to elevate their vision or idea to a whole new level of bigger and better. The Extraordinary Gap's effect becomes far more challenging when a Founder launches or grows their business. In these times of growth, the Founder's vision is most vulnerable to sliding into the reality of the ordinary. In some cases, the Extraordinary Gap becomes so wide that it creates a phenomenon I call "Founder-Settling."

FOUNDER-SETTLING

Founder-Settling is a form of disillusionment that happens to Founders with high-flying, fast-moving, and big visions. There are two main drivers of Founder-Settling. The first is obvious; the second is a little trickier to see. The first driver occurs when a Founder must simplify their visions so the "average" person can understand them. Or when they feel the need to adjust their vision significantly because it's the only way for reality to be achieved. An even worse example is when Employees start to interpret the Founder's vision to their level of reality and unknowingly widen the gap even more.

The second driver of Founder-Settling typically is most prevalent in the "middle phase" of when a Founder is actually in the process of transforming their vision into reality. The middle phase is the most challenging phase for everyone in the company, unlike the starting phase of the company or expanding phase of the company.

The middle phase is when everyone stops talking about the company's possibilities or the company's growth and starts to do the work to make it happen. It's when the Employees transform the Founder's extraordinary vision into action plans, projects, and budgets. The Employees now take the Founder's concept and stretch, pull, and reshape it to bring it to life. Employees are making decisions on what will work and what will not.

Employees get excited in the middle phase because even though it is hard work, they can see how their work is transforming the Founder's vision into reality. Founder-Settling is a little trickier for Employees to see in the middle phase because as they are excited about the work, the Founder sees their ultimate vision go from grandeur to ordinary.

It's super important to note that even when the Employees accomplish something extraordinary, there is always some type of gap between the Employee's vision of extraordinary and the Founder's vision of extraordinary.

FOUNDER-SETTLING PHASES

Phase	Start	Middle	Expanding
Founder's Emotion	Excitement	Disillusionment	Enthusiasm
Founder's Vision	Vision is Crystal Clear	Vision is slipping into the Ordinary	A New Vision is Born

THE THREE STATES OF DISILLUSIONMENT

How does Founder-Settling impact you? Typically, when the Founder starts to settle, three predominant states of disillusionment appear. When you see these states, you will quickly know just how big an Extraordinary Gap exists between the Founder and you, the team, or the business. Still, even in these states, there are plenty of opportunities to be an impact player.

1. **Withdrawal.** The Founder cannot stand looking at the business in a less-than-perfect vision state, so they begin to withdraw. They stop showing up physically, emotionally, or even intellectually. They lose their passion for the vision because they see it sliding to ordinary, and they do the minimum of what is necessary to contribute.

   How This Looks to YOU: The Founder disconnects. There is little excitement shown for any forward progress. The Founder is no longer spending hours and hours poring over the project or accepting updates with enthusiasm. It's as if their heart is broken, and they are just suffering through, unable to stop their disconnection, and are uninspired to move forward.

2. **Push.** The Founder begins to push Employees to extreme levels of expectations. At times, the Founder becomes very vocal, even verbally abusive, out of the perceived incremental destruction of their business and the harsh realization that what the Founder once saw as exciting and new has become nothing but

ordinary. The Founder "doubles down" against letting their vision slip and makes the team pay the price for the slip to the mundane.

How This Looks to YOU: You feel an extreme push to elevate the project from the ordinary and to push it with everything you have to get it back to extraordinary. Everything you bring gets rejected until the Founder accepts it. Nothing else matters, and there are no more significant priorities until the project returns to a level of extraordinary. You are pushed to the edge, to the brink of exhaustion, to close the Extraordinary Gap.

3. **Reconsideration.** The Founder starts questioning the validity of their vision. Was it too much? Was it before its time? Was it just too complicated? As the Extraordinary Gap begins to expand, the Founder begins to question whether the business is really "for" them or if they are really meant for the company. Or, the Founder begins to question their leadership because "clearly no one understands." The Founder becomes fraught with doubt, questions, and concerns about where they are and wonders if this was all just too much. At this point, it's a crapshoot. The Founder may withdraw, push harder, delay, or start over.

How This Looks to YOU: Everything you and the team have worked on is thrown into the proverbial garbage can. (Note: You will do well to never throw anything out with a Founder; you never know when you will be asked for it again.) The Founder decides to start over, and everyone needs to rethink, rework, and reassess from the beginning with a new and improved vision. You must quickly shift gears to the new concept and never again mention the old vision until the Founder brings it up.

EMBRACE YOUR GENIUS

THREE STEPS FOR YOU TO CLOSE THE EXTRAORDINARY GAP

Here are three ways for you to thrive with a Founder who appears to be suffering from the disillusionment of slipping into the ordinary.

1. Recognize the importance of continuing to fulfill your responsibilities to your job. Imagine if the entire team stopped or slowed down every time a Founder became disillusioned—the business would never gain any success traction.

2. Acknowledge that Founders are human. Sometimes they need a little time to reconcile the gap between their vision and reality, especially in the middle phase. The key here is to acknowledge the simple fact that the middle phase may seem ordinary, yet it is a necessary step to transform the Founder's vision into reality. The middle phase is not the end of the game; it's only the middle, and there is still a lot of the game to play and greatness to appear.

3. Try to work with the Founder to stay aligned with their vision. In my experience, this is where real

innovation happens. Think about ways to align with the Founder versus challenging or chipping away at the Founder's vision. It is easy to "simplify" a vision. It is far more exciting and valuable to innovate a solution to perpetuate a Founder's vision and move out of the middle of the ordinary and back on the path to extraordinary.

DEATH BY INCREMENTALISM

Founder-Settling often leads to a second phenomenon I refer to as "death by incrementalism." In other words, it's not the one big decision that impacts a Founder's vision. It's the hundreds of small decisions that, when taken together, shift the Founder's mindset from their extraordinary vision to disillusionment.

Often, Employees misinterpret these "little or less meaningful" decisions as the Founder's "quirky issues." (This is where words like "crazy," "picky," or "unhappy" enter the conversation.) Employees see such decisions as little, while the Founder sees them as a continued expansion of the Extraordinary Gap.

When this happens in a company, statements start to circulate, such as, "Be careful, the Founder is in a mood today because they did not get what they wanted." Unfortunately, most Employees miss entirely that the Founder sees all these little incremental decisions as the beginning of the end. The Founder's mind can begin to spiral out of control over incrementalism. At a certain point, even the smallest decision can launch a full-blown slide, leading to such worst-case scenarios as going bankrupt, losing their house, disassociating from family and friends, and ultimately seeing their dreams become nightmares.

Employees consistently miss the culminating effects of all these little decisions/shifts/changes as they occur and keep moving forward. As a result, the little things go unnoticed for the Employees and become small "cuts" to the Founder. This ultimately causes the brilliant vision to fall victim to death by incrementalism.

THE POWER OF INNOVATION TO CLOSE THE EXTRAORDINARY GAP

Your success is accelerated when you master the difference between incrementalism and innovation. Incrementalism subtracts from a Founder's vision. Incrementalism is the act of shifting, adjusting, and changing against the Founder's will. The Founder believes that their vision is being distorted or, in some cases, destroyed. The Founder reluctantly concedes to the changes. Founders do not find this process inspiring.

Innovation is when changes or modifications are being made to the Founder's vision, which adds more value, efficiency, or brilliance to the vision. Founders get excited and engaged in innovation, a very different experience from incrementalism. They become energized by changes that move their vision to new levels.

The easiest way for you to know the difference between incrementalism and innovation is a Founder's response to the change. If the Founder is excited, energized, and accepting of the suggested changes, this is innovation. If the Founder is defensive, resistant, and reluctantly agrees to go along with the changes, this is incrementalism. The table below will help you identify the differences between incrementalism and innovation related to your Founder's response.

Founder's Responses to Incrementalism	Founder's Responses to Innovation
"I wonder if any of these suggestions really add any real value."	"This is a terrific idea—how can we move forward with it?"
"Let's just take another look at this to make sure we have addressed all options."	"What will be the impact in three years?"
"How far did we move away from the original vision?"	"This is a great way of making things happen!"
"Who else can I discuss this with to make sure we are not being extreme?"	"Let's challenge ourselves to think outside the box even more—we are on the right path!"
"Do you really think it is a good idea to make this change?"	"This change will move everything forward for the better. Fantastic!"

Embrace Your Genius

Identifying the Difference between Incrementalism and Innovation

Your greatest opportunity is to manage the middle process while navigating through the fine lines of innovation and incrementalism. It is essential to realize that you are managing three codependent paths: holding the Founder's vision, minimizing incrementalism, and maximizing innovation. All of this while, of course, still grinding it out every day to make the Founder's dream a reality. Here are some key points for you to manage through the middle phase.

When making decisions that deviate from the Founder's vision, ask yourself the following questions:

- What is the ultimate goal for both the Founder and business to bring an extraordinary idea to reality? How does your decision or direction add value?
- What is the size of the gap between the Founder's vision and the reality of your current situation if your recommendation or decision is implemented?
- How much push are you getting from your Founder on new ideas? The greater the push, the greater the need for you to innovate. Less push means you are on the right path. Keep checking in for clarity and alignment. The no push or no

comment signals your Founder has disengaged from the process.

Leverage the innovative process to challenge and stretch your own creative thinking. Sometimes innovation occurs when you challenge your own thought process. Think about innovation as your process to keep the Founder's vision 100 percent whole while taking the project to a whole new level of possibilities.

Challenge yourself to break out of your "comfort zone." Innovation allows you to think "outside the box" or to let go of conventional wisdom. It's your time to be bold, brave, and bring new innovative ideas to your Founder.

The Extraordinary Gap is shared by both Founders and Employees in terms of sheer frustration and excitement. It's the power of that gap that pushes both Founders and Employees to stretch past the ordinary to the extraordinary. Think about all the possibilities for you and your Founder to skip incrementalism and accelerate innovation.

Love Your Journey

Stop

- ✗ Dismissing the Founder's vision as being unrealistic or impossible to achieve
- ✗ Being frustrated by the Founder's constant push for the extraordinary
- ✗ Disengaging when you are in the middle phase just because your Founder is disengaged

Start

- ❯ Pushing for closer alignment to the Founder's vision in the middle phase
- ❯ Striving for possibilities and keeping your Founder engaged
- ❯ Stretching yourself for innovation over incrementalism

WOODISM

"The Employee is the reflection of the Leader — push to reflect the extraordinary in all of us."

The Epicenter of Crisis
SUCCESS PRACTICE 10

*It doesn't matter whether a Founder starts in
freeze, flight, or fight mode in a crisis. All that
matters is where the Founder finishes.*

FOUNDEROLOGY **REALITY**

The year 2020 was an unforgettable year everyone would likely just as soon forget. The world as we knew it changed immediately and forever in what many called repeatedly "unprecedented times." If the word "unprecedented" had been part of a worldwide drinking game, most of the world would've been drunk. However, this was not a drinking game. The world was in a global pandemic as the deadly invisible Coronavirus (COVID-19) wreaked havoc on lives, livelihoods, countries, economies, and our entire planet. Within weeks of first being detected, COVID-19 changed everything, and not for the better. Millions lost their jobs, and many Founders watched their businesses go from busy to gone.

Every aspect of daily life was impacted. Many would say that COVID-19 was the worst thing that ever happened to them, as they became ill, or worse, lost a loved one to the virus. People also experienced other losses such as their jobs, their homes, and the discontinuation of life event celebrations (birthdays, anniversaries, graduations, weddings, etc.).

The immediate short-term impact was real, raw, and jarring. The long-term impact of shutting down, shutting off, and shuttering in the entire world's population will take years, if not decades, for us to fully comprehend.

The COVID-19 pandemic stretched Founders in so many directions. It took massive tolls on themselves, their teams, customers, and communities. As a Founder of two businesses myself, I saw my livelihood go from being on pace for record-breaking revenue to both companies going to zero before coming back to full operations. In my consulting practice, my clients and colleagues across the United States were on what I called the COVID Continuum. The scale ran from negative cash positions to positive cash positions and everything in between.

Many Founders will say that COVID-19 dashed their dreams, robbing them of their business and ruining their life's purpose. Many others will say COVD-19 was a benefit to them, a blessing in disguise. They found more time to spend with family, friends, and in their community (even wearing a mask and practicing social-distancing guidelines) while participating in activities they usually would not have otherwise.

Many Founders found more time to reflect on their life's purpose, engaging in more comfortable, less stressful ways to live, spending more time in nature, taking up new hobbies, and rediscovering activities long forgotten. Employees found themselves in similar positions as Founders, with both challenges and opportunities. Many businesses innovated new ideas, products, and services. Founders and Employees rekindled new passions, energy, and purpose to pursue their business dreams becoming a reality.

Find Your Sanity

Crises in any form have and will always be a part of life and business. As the saying goes, "You have to break down before you can break through." Of course, there were many breakdowns during COVID-19 from the devastating loss of so many loved ones, businesses, jobs, and canceled life events.

Breakthroughs became a massive part of the COVID-19 pandemic. One of the single most incredible breakthroughs was the development of vaccines in record-breaking time. John F. Kennedy had a great quote about a crisis: "In a crisis, be aware of the danger, but recognize the opportunity."

Many Founder-led businesses experienced breakthroughs that accelerated their business growth and opportunities for expansion. No matter the crisis, what will always remain true is that Founders must decide in moments of crisis to view them as danger or as a unique opportunity for change and improvement.

FOUNDERS RESPONSE TO CRISIS

In studying acute stress response—how a person responds to a crisis—early twentieth-century American physiologist Walter Bradford Cannon coined the term "fight or flight response." In the years since, physiologists and psychologists have continued to build on and refine Cannon's work. They've come to a greater understanding of how people react to a crisis using what is called "freeze, flight, or fight response." Founders and most people generally react and handle crises with one of these three responses.

	FREEZE	FLIGHT	FIGHT
ACTION in CRISIS	Stop; Dig In	Chase; Run	Lead; Plan and Act

Think about this for a minute. When you are in any crisis, what is your immediate response—freeze, flight, or fight? If you can identify your response ahead of time, it will be easier to work with your Founder as you learn their response. A key to successfully getting through a crisis is understanding what your "go-to" response is to a crisis and how it aligns with your Founder's go-to response.

FOUNDERS
MUST DECIDE
in moments of crisis to view them as danger or
AS A UNIQUE
OPPORTUNITY
FOR CHANGE AND
IMPROVEMENT.

Dealing with a crisis is an equal opportunity event for everyone involved.

I realized early in my career that my response to a crisis was to fight. My fight response allows me to evaluate all opportunities that I think will make the situation better by fighting. Knowing my response is essential for me to calibrate my response with my clients' and Employees' responses when leading them through a crisis. Knowing where everyone is on the scale will help move you and your Founder forward in any type of crisis.

READING A FOUNDER'S CRISIS RESPONSE

When a crisis threatens a Founder's business, there is an immediate instinctual reaction of Freeze, Flight, or Fight in responding to the threat with a range of consequences. The range of consequences extends from the loss of sales, Employees, and customers to loss of business and even the remote possibility of ending up homeless on a park bench. Please note any loss for a Founder is considered a threat to their business. Let's examine each of these three responses relative to how a Founder approaches a crisis and what it means to you.

FOUNDERS IN FREEZE

Countless psychological journal articles have been published on why humans freeze in moments of extreme stress. A Founder with a freeze response is stuck, like a deer in the headlights. They have lost their compass and their natural will to move forward. A frozen Founder will exhibit some of the following attributes:

- confused and overwhelmed
- sense of impending doom
- stressed to the point of paralysis
- withdrawn and non-responsive
- communication is virtually non-existent
- physical symptoms of extreme anxiety, anxiousness, depression, and so on

Founders with a freeze response can talk themselves into believing many of the following:

- "If I just don't move, things will get better."
- "Someone or something will come and rescue me."
- "If I move, I might make it worse than it is."
- "It is better to wait than to be reckless."
- "This is why I have a team that can deal with this mess."

Having a Founder who exhibits a freeze response in a crisis limits how much anyone can be helped in and out of the crisis. A frozen Founder is limited in their ability to inspire confidence in Employees that success is just around the corner. I have worked with many Founders who respond to a crisis by freezing. It is not so much a judgment of them and their capabilities; it just shows they are human like the rest of us.

A frozen Founder will not initially lead a company out of the crisis. Ultimately, they almost always move back into their leadership role and fight for their business as they start to get unstuck.

EMBRACE YOUR GENIUS

HOW TO SUPPORT A FOUNDER IN FREEZE

You have many options when you see your Founder in freeze mode.

- 💡 Realize the crisis is still happening, even if the Founder wants it to be over.
- 💡 The best option for inaction is action, especially in a crisis. Take the initiative. Gather the team, develop a plan, share the plan with the Founder, and start moving yourself and the team forward.
- 💡 Don't call the Founder out on their obvious freeze response. Try to bring the Founder into your discussions, conversations, and plans to move forward; this helps Founders start to move again.

FOUNDERS IN FLIGHT

Founders in flight mode may chase after new opportunities daily, even hourly, with each opportunity enthusiastically endorsed and promoted by the Founder until the next idea. A Founder in flight chases after hundreds of ideas in a time of crisis, with the notion that maybe one will strike real gold.

Remember *Shiny Object Syndrome* from earlier in the book? This is how it plays out again. In a moment of crisis, the Founder takes shiny object syndrome and multiplies it by a thousand, as if the shiny object syndrome is on steroids.

The Founder will rationalize their behavior as necessary because they are wired to save the company, save jobs, and support the community. Who can dispute that logic? Who knows, the Founder may land on one idea that could be a home run and save the entire company!

Founders' in-flight responses are adrenaline-fueled "GO" responses that make it nearly impossible for them to tire out. They can escalate very quickly to that point because, again, it's another part of their DNA to be creative, innovative, and a rule breaker. It is their natural inclination to try new things, explore multiple options, and blaze new trails. These are all amazing things about a Founder most of the time, yet they make it some of the most challenging things about a Founder in crisis. Founders in flight mode can look like the following:

- Setting a new direction for the business every day.
- Generating a constant flow of new ideas and acting on most of them.
- Trying "get quick" ideas, confident they will help the business.
- Buying equipment or things the company does not need.
- Non-stop discussions about all solutions.

Founders in flight mode benefit significantly by being forced to stop and look at the validity of their actual results. It's a question of, "Are my actions truly producing any results that are positively impacting the business?" Sure, Founders in flight mode are busy, but are they being effective? Is anything being accomplished? What is the current focus of the business when a Founder is in flight response?

EMBRACE YOUR GENIUS

HOW TO SUPPORT A FOUNDER IN FLIGHT

Working with a Founder in flight mode through a crisis can be exhilarating, exhausting, and completely unpredictable. If you love fast action, constant change, and unpredictability, this is a fantastic experience to witness a Founder's creative process speed. My advice to Employees working with a Founder in flight mode is to strategically present reality to the Founder to help them see the results of all their actions. These are some of my tried-and-true recommendations for Employees to help Founders see their actions and their results more clearly.

- Keep a running total of all the projects your Founder is currently working on or has presented. A Founder in flight mode will have a pretty long list. A Founder seeing the list is often enough to slow the pace down to focus on priorities.

- Present the project list to your Founder and ask them to work with you to prioritize them from:
  - highest to lowest probability for success
  - profitable to least profitable
  - immediate impact versus long-term impact
  - most relevant to your current business strategies versus farthest away from your existing business strategies
- Review the list with your Founder and start making decisions on which priorities will genuinely impact the business in ways that are most helpful in moving the company from crisis to stability.
- Ask your Founder if you can:
  - set up weekly meetings to review and report on only the top three priorities
  - keep track of all new projects and ideas versus having to drop everything and start something new every other day
- Another recommendation I have made to Employees is to discuss with the Founder when to declare the business is no longer in crisis. One thing about a crisis is that it's never permanent, even if the news says that there is still a crisis. You and your Founder can decide it's no longer a crisis for your business, and then it's time to stop just surviving and start thriving. Yes, the crisis may persist, yet you all have a choice for how long you want it to persist as a paralyzing force in the business.

Founders in flight mode may not readily express their gratitude to you. They will be grateful for the disruption of their activities and for the opportunity to stop, breathe, and reassess the situation in a less chaotic state. Even if they never say anything, their focused actions and shorter lists of priorities will say it all.

FOUNDERS IN FIGHT

Founders in fight mode are "in it to win it." They are driven by the idea that the crisis will not beat them. They will attack the crisis and come out stronger and better for themselves, the team, the community, and the business. They are committed to the core of their being that conquering the crisis is just another hurdle in their path for success. Founders in fight will run into a crisis to knock it down. They are very confident the crisis will not knock them down.

In times of crisis, we hear and read countless stories about businesses downsizing, laying off Employees, and altogether failing. The statistics on failed businesses are unbelievably negative and, quite honestly, very difficult to always read about. At the same time, in the same crisis, there are countless stories of Founders and companies thriving, achieving sales records and profitability goals, and scaling new heights of success, all with great teams of dedicated and committed Employees.

How do Founders in the fight move forward, successfully navigating the unpredictability of a crisis? The answer is they are driven to put predictability into the unpredictable. They are of the mindset that there is always an opportunity in every crisis—it is an intentional choice.

Founders in fight mode are focused, committed, and driven to rise to the challenge of making their business successful in a crisis environment. They are agile, flexible, and adaptable, continuously evolving their business to meet their customers' needs and their business balance sheet. They are inspired to evaluate and innovate their business and to lead their teams with confidence so they will all win.

A Founder in fight mode looks:
- focused and determined
- agile and flexible
- attentive; they listen and ask questions
- innovative and inclusive
- realistic and pragmatic
- confident; they leverage their network, business, and Employees for the fight

Founders in fight mode are driven by the true purpose of their business. It isn't just about the business surviving the crisis and simply making it. It's a greater calling of why their business needs to make it, because its purpose is more significant than just making money.

Many Founders believe that the purpose of their company can positively impact and change the world. They are not out to rescue the world as much as be a part of creating a world that is stronger, better, and healthier for all. Working for a Founder in fight mode is not always all rainbows and sunshine. There are challenging days, difficult conversations, and rough struggles that seem to never end. However, a Founder in fight mode accepts this as part of the journey and moves forward despite it all.

EMBRACE YOUR GENIUS

HOW TO SUPPORT A FOUNDER IN FIGHT

Working with a Founder in fight mode can be a life-changing experience for you personally and professionally. You are part of a business that never says never—it charges forth each day to kick it in the ass before it kicks their ass. How can you succeed with a Founder in the fight? Here are a few tips to consider:

- Shift your mindset—focus on possibilities versus impossibilities
- Learn to accept change as a way of moving the business forward
- Develop your abilities to be flexible, adaptable, and agile
- Don't be afraid to speak up even when you don't have all the answers or confidence
- Get in the ring and fight beside your Founder to achieve greatness for the business

There is a great quote by Ray Kroc, Founder of McDonald's, that I think is perfect when fighting a crisis: "The only way to control your destiny is to create it." Founders in fight mode do just that—they are taking control of their destiny. Rather than letting the crisis run rampant over their business and define their outcome of success or failure, they accept the crisis, embrace the moment, and act, refusing to be defined by it. It's not the easiest path to take. Still, it can be one of the most critical paths to take in a crisis.

Crisis events put a spotlight on how you and your Founder respond under pressure—how the Founder responds and how you respond. There is no right or wrong response; it's all about how we are wired as people. Think about your response to a crisis. How has your response helped you to survive or thrive in life and business? What can you learn from your Founder or about your response that will support you in leading, navigating, and managing through crises in life and business? Sometimes even in crisis, we are given the gift of greater understanding and humanity as we work together for better days.

Love Your Journey

Stop

- ❌ Reacting to the drama of the crisis
- ❌ Living in the doom of the crisis
- ❌ Investing time speculating on all the potential downsides of the crisis

Start

- ❯ Focusing on moving the company out of crisis
- ❯ Understanding your response to crisis and your relationship to your Founder's response to crisis
- ❯ Being flexible and agile as a crisis is continuously changing

WOODISM

"A crisis is a traumatic catalyst that can be leveraged to create unity, community, and embrace the good in humanity."

Founderology 201
TWO BRIDGES OF FEAR AND FAITH

The strongest bridge is the one of faith.

FOUNDEROLOGY REALITY

A Founder, Manager, and Employee enter a large green room.

The Founder says, "This is amazing. Look at this—nothing but green fields for me to create and grow so many things. I can't wait!"

The Manager, with a deep breath, a slight eye roll, and a feeling of *here we go again,* says, "I will develop systems and processes to support everything you want to create and grow."

The Employee says, "Respectfully, are you both crazy? Who is going to cut all this grass?"

THE BRIDGE OF FAITH BETWEEN FOUNDERS AND EMPLOYEES

Like most Founders and Employees, I tend to search for answers everywhere, in both easy and challenging times.

In my journey, I have learned that when my fear is at its highest, I must look to my faith for the answers. When I speak of faith, Founders and Employees immediately assume I am talking about spiritual faith and tune out or declare this is not an appropriate conversation for business.

Faith is entirely appropriate in business because what I am focusing on are mindsets and beliefs. When people tell me we can't talk faith, I double down, even more determined to have the conversation. It's not about discussing religion as much about having faith and confidence in the strength of the company's core. Here are a few essentials in every company's core:

- Purpose, vision, and mission of the company
- Founder
- Employees
- Concept and its potential
- Growth plans and their possibilities
- Customers and connectivity
- Community involvement

The stronger the core, the stronger the faith everyone has in each other and the business. Sometimes the core can be shaken, tested, and challenged as a company grows. It's why I developed my concept of the "Two Bridges" that I share with both Founders and Employees.

Two Bridges - Fear and Faith

I believe Founders and Employees have two bridges to choose from when building a great business. One is the bridge of fear; the other is the bridge of faith. Failure is a part of both. There is a condition known as gephyrophobia. It is a condition that causes people to have an intense fear of crossing a bridge; even the mere thought or anticipation of it can bring on panic attacks.

Gephyrophobes are not worried about the bridge collapsing. They are very concerned about themselves collapsing on the bridge. Think about this for a moment with you and your Founder when you are about to take the next step in growing the business, doing something completely new, or introducing profound change. What bridge are you on: fear or faith?

I can tell when both Founders and Employees are on the bridge of fear by their response to change, innovation, or stepping out of their comfort zone. Founders and Employees make statements like:
- "That will never work here."
- "We tried that in 1960. It didn't work then. Why would it work now?"
- "Why do we even need to do this?"
- "This is crazy!"
- And my personal favorite, usually said by a very passionate Employee: "I am just playing devil's advocate and would like to present an opposite point of view."

I am always grateful when a Founder or Employee declares they are the devil's advocate. At this point, I know immediately they are on the bridge of fear and are opposed to any change. How am I so confident their position is on the bridge of fear? Think about this— do angels have advocates? Why would someone be advocating for the devil? Being the devil's advocate is just another way of saying, "I disagree, and I will stay on the bridge of fear, stopping everything from moving forward."

What drives Founders and Employees to choose the bridge of fear? In my experience, it has been everything from fear of failure to being extremely fatigued and everything in between. However, no matter the reason, the result is always the same—no one and nothing moves forward. Like with Gephyrophobes, the higher the goal or the more significant the challenge, the more the fear and paralysis persist.

On the bridge of faith, failure serves to be a catalyst to dig deeper and keep moving forward. However, failure is not what keeps Founders and Employees on the bridge of faith. What keeps Founders and Employees on the bridge of faith is the trilogy for success—belief, confidence, and the greatest one of them all, trust in their core. Walt Disney captured this trilogy best when he said, "If you can dream it, you can do it!" The bridge of faith is fueled by trust between the Founder and Employees and their shared commitment to something greater than themselves.

I love the word "trust" when working with Founders and Employees on the bridge of faith. Lack of trust is the common denominator that destroys all teams, businesses, and relationships. It also is a catalyst for moving Founders and Employees onto the bridge of fear. Let's take a closer look at the concept of trust to see its power on the bridge of faith.

If you remove the first "t" from trust, you get the word "rust." Rust is an interesting chemical reaction because it typically starts small and is barely noticeable. Over time, if not addressed, the rust will worsen and continually erode and weaken structures, essentially spreading until the object is no longer useful.

What erodes and destroys a team? A lack of trust. If you don't address trust issues between a Founder and Employees, over time, just like rust, it erodes the entire team and business. You can see the impact a lack of trust has in everyday life, in business, sports, politics (for sure!), and even in relationships.

When you trust your Founder, it translates to believing in their vision and the confidence to make that vision a reality. Also, when the Founder trusts you, it leads to greater confidence and collaboration. The one word in the middle of trust is "US"—Founders and Employees. When both you and your Founder have a bond of trust, a powerful bridge of faith is built between you and your Founder.

Founders and Employees who thrive together are all on the same bridge of faith, believing in something greater than themselves. Many cynics will say, "Yes, they're bridged together by a big payout." I think we would all agree that a payout or financial reward is a fantastic incentive and great recognition for everyone's hard work and commitment.

I have found, though, that genuinely committed Founders and Employees who succeed are driven more by creating and building something that will change the world, solve a problem, or just bring a moment of happiness to someone's day. Their shared drive is inspired by a collective faith in their core of purpose, vision, and mission to impact the world, large or small.

EMBRACE YOUR GENIUS

MOVING FORWARD ON THE BRIDGE OF FAITH

I have always been grateful to my core for the Founders and Employees who have had faith in my vision, abilities, and passion for working with them to make their visions a reality.

Employees' faith can get tested many times in a Founder-led business. It can be tested for so many reasons, personally and professionally. My advice to Employees to keep moving forward when tested is to strengthen their position on the bridge of faith. These are practices I suggest for gaining more strength:

- Take ten minutes, whether it be a quiet morning or a planned day off, and reset your balance between your goals and the goals of your Founder.
- Talk with your Founder and reconnect with their vision and passion. Use it as a catalyst for you. Do a check of your thinking/feelings compared to where their reality is and their stressors, so you can better understand their perspective.
- Refresh your faith, whether in family, friends, your dreams, or in other ways you find inspiration. Write about it, talk about it, and keep moving it forward.

TOUCHSTONES FOR STAYING ON THE BRIDGE OF FAITH

Over the years, I have shared with Founders and Employees the touchstones I have relied on to help lessen my fear and amplify my faith in myself, my team, and my businesses throughout my journey. These touchstones have calmed my mind, strengthened my confidence, and inspired me to move toward a brighter day.

Even on the darkest days of being knocked down by failure more times than I can count, I have always been raised up by my faith in all the possibilities of the universe. I share these touchstones so you and your Founder can stay on the bridge of faith to move forward. As I like to say, "It may sound crazy to do the impossible. That's why we must have faith in the possible in our core."

I firmly believe successful Founders and Employees all have touchstones to help them through the good, bad, challenging, unbearable, and most exciting days. Touchstones give Founders and Employees something to serve as a beacon of light in the winds and storms of change to stay on the bridge of faith.

I share these with you so you might use these or find your own touchstones, and you can continue to thrive with any boss, in any workplace, and in any aspect of your life.

Asking for Help

Great Founders and Employees ask for what they want, seek what they need, and knock-on thousands of doors for opportunities!

Ask for help, not because you are weak, but because you want to remain strong.
— Les Brown

You are never strong enough that you don't need help.
— Cesar Chavez

BELIEVING

Founders and Employees are not alone in their journeys. Everyone has the choice to believe and engage their heads, hearts, and hands to excel in an entrepreneurial world.

Dear optimist, pessimist, and realist—while you guys were busy arguing about the glass of wine, I drank it! Sincerely, the opportunist!
— Lori Greiner

If you don't like the road you're walking, start paving another one.
— Dolly Parton

CLARITY OF VISION

When we lose our vision, we lose our direction. My leadership philosophy is: "The clearer the leader, the clearer the team."When Founders and Employees struggle, it is time to step back and check their vision.

If you can dream it, you can do it.
— Walt Disney

I am not afraid; I was made for this.
— Joan of Arc

COMMITMENT

When Founders and Employees leverage power, love, and a shared vision, they can transform fear into faith. They can all step onto the bridge of faith and walk forward.

> *Bring your whole self to all you do—anything less shortchanges you and your possibilities.*
> — Fritzi Woods

> *I've learned that fear limits you and your vision. It serves as blinders to what may be just a few steps down the road for you. The journey is valuable, but believing in your talents, your abilities, and your self-worth can empower you to walk down an even brighter path. Transforming fear into freedom—how great is that?*
> — Soledad O'Brien

COURAGE

The word "courage" comes from the French word *corag,* which translates to "heart." It takes a lot of heart for Founders and Employees to thrive together—the courage to have difficult conversations, persevere in challenging times, and continue to thrive together, paving new success paths.

The credit belongs to the man who is actually in the arena; whose face is marred with dust and sweat; who strives valiantly, who errs and may fall again and again because there is no effort without error or shortcoming.
— Theodore Roosevelt

If you are also not in the arena getting your ass kicked, I am not interested in getting your feedback.
— Brené Brown

TRUST

Trust is the cornerstone for all strong, healthy, vibrant, and thriving relationships. Without trust, our relationships will rust.

Trust is the glue of life. It's the most essential ingredient in effective communication. It's the foundational principle that holds all relationships.
— Stephen Covey

Love all, trust a few, do wrong to none.
— William Shakespeare

GRATITUDE
The art of being thankful.

Success is a journey filled with failure, so accept them both.
— Unknown

*You are never too old or too young to pursue your dream,
and always move forward with more faith than fear.*
— Kathleen Wood

LOVE YOUR JOURNEY

My final thought for you is one of gratitude. Thank you for reading all the way to the end of *Founderology*. Thank you for doing what you do every day to make our world a better place. Thank you for your commitment to success with any Founder in any workplace. Some may say you are crazy, and I would say you are crazy enough to change the world. Be crazy—Find Your Sanity, Embrace Your Genius, and Love Your Journey!

Kathleen

Kathleen Wood's Founder Journey

Founders are what I call the unicorns of business. They are risk-takers who are willing to do whatever it takes to make their dreams a reality. Founders are the ones who can see a bright future while everyone else just sees a single light bulb. They will be revered, vilified, honored, criticized, and frequently misunderstood. It has been my pleasure to work with amazing Founders and their teams for over twenty years.

I understand Founders because I founded my growth strategy consulting firm, Kathleen Wood Partners, over two decades ago. Today, Kathleen Wood Partners specializes in working with great people who want to grow great brands. We work with Founders in the areas of strategic growth planning, business optimization, competitive brand development, and leadership development.

My consulting practice has provided me amazing opportunities to work side by side with Founders and their Employees across the United States and internationally, all with a shared mission to make their visions a reality.

I have so much gratitude for all the Founders and Employees I have worked with through the years as we have developed strategic plans, business and brand optimization processes, and leadership development programs. All these efforts transformed small companies into market leaders, award-winners, and even billion-dollar brands.

I am also grateful for all the opportunities to consult with large publicly traded companies that were looking for innovative strategies to expand and diversify their portfolio. Kathleen Wood Partners continues to be a great journey today as we actively engage with Founders and Employees in food service, restaurants, hospitality, technology, healthcare, manufacturing, professional services, and any other type of business where the Founder is committed to seeing their vision become a successful reality.

At the time I started Kathleen Wood Partners, I can honestly say taking the corporate path was the far more popular route for most of my colleagues. I realized that one of my strongest superpowers was my ability to clearly see how to build and grow businesses on the most productive and profitable paths possible. I had accomplished this repeatedly in my corporate life, and I was ready to do it in my own entrepreneurial life. I took the path less traveled to help, support, and lead others to create their own Founder's path for success. I was, as I like to say, the guru of a gig economy before the gig economy was even trendy.

As Kathleen Wood Partners continued to grow as a leading growth strategy firm, an exciting personal dream for me was realized with my sister Sue and her daughters, Jen and Julie, when we opened our family-owned and operated business, Suzy's Swirl. Together we developed, created, and opened Suzy's Swirl, a frozen dessert shop dedicated to providing one million moments of *Frozen Happiness* for our customers and community.

We, as a family, have journeyed many paths of success, trial, and failure, and through it all, we have stayed committed to making the world a sweeter place with Suzy's Swirl. We have been blessed with loyal, dedicated, and hard-working Managers and crew members who have truly supported us all in transforming our vision into reality. Today, Sue leads Suzy's Swirl and our continued commitment of *Swirling* Goodness in our product, *Swirling Greatness* with our team, and *Swirling Gratitude* for our crew, customers, and community.

For most of my career, I was simply called crazy—crazy to work with so many Founders who all shared a common goal of growing their businesses into the next great brand. Crazy for starting a family-owned business as Kathleen Wood Partners was expanding. These Founders' journeys and my family's business journey all form the tapestry of my Founder's journey. I speak the unspoken language of Founders and the translation of it for Employees. I intrinsically understand the good, the bad, and the ugly of starting and growing a business for both Founders and Employees.

It takes a Founder to know a Founder and personally know the power of Founders and Employees working toward a shared vision. Many might even say *Founderology* is my autobiography on some levels, both as a Founder and an Employee. I am proud to be the Founder of Kathleen Wood Partners, Suzy's Swirl, and, I am sure, many more companies to follow. I am excited to share *Founderology* with the purpose of making it possible for both Founders and Employees to find their sanity, embrace their genius, and love their journey together!

Kathleen

Acknowledgments

I am thankful to every amazing Employee who worked in the same Founder-led businesses that I consulted, led, and still lead today. Without their dedication, passion, and tenacity, many of the companies that we admire today would have never happened. I truly do believe that Founders always have the vision, and Employees are the heart and soul of a business. I have always respected and admired Employees for their amazing efforts and sometimes extraordinary sacrifices and commitments to make the vision a reality.

I am very grateful to all the brilliant Founders I have had the pleasure to work with over the past two decades and continue with today. I thank them for the opportunity to have worked with them on their strategic path for taking their visions and making them a reality. It has been and continues to be an honor to work, literally sometimes all day and all night, in the pursuit of growing their amazing companies and brands. It has also been a joy to see the growth and impact of their businesses even after our work together was done.

With *Swirling Gratitude,* I want to thank our team at Suzy's Swirl, our family business. I am grateful for the many amazing *Swirlers* who started with us as crew members and who are and will be the next generation of great leaders. I am thankful for every day and every hour they committed to our shared vision of inspiring one million moments of frozen happiness, one cup at a time. Specically, I want to give *Swirling Thanks* to Jen Tierno, Julie Tierno, Caitlyn Keefe, Laine McKnight, Jenelle Frevert, and Abigail Frea, for their leadership, passion, and unwavering belief in our shared vision.

Additionally, I would like to express *Swirling Gratitude* to Joe Tierno, Jim Tierno, Joe and Lucy Tierno, Keegan Tierno, Mary and Kerry Caba, Brian Caba, and Courtney Caba Siragusa for all of their love and unwavering belief in Suzy's Swirl.

I will be forever grateful to all of my inspiring and amazing friends who have supported me in the many journeys of my career path working with Founders and Employees. Special thanks to Jim Knight, Jamie Griffin, Lyn Magnarini, Marla Topliff, Anna Mason, Julie Ophiem, Brant Menswar, Sam Stanovich, Sandy Korem, Jennie Stenback, Dave Place, Lisa Wolf, Edna Morris, Joanna Rolek, Joleen Goronkin, Margie McCartney, and Hope Van Fleet for your direct feedback, collaboration, friendship, and support. Your insights and wisdom were perfectly timed in this process. Special thanks to Elizabeth McCormick and her team for helping me always fly right with *Founderology*.

Most importantly, I am so grateful for my business partner and sister, Sue Tierno. She didn't set out to be a Founder; to her credit, she has become a great one. On our journey with Suzy's Swirl, she has been my greatest inspiration for family, faith, and fun in building our family business. She kept the faith when we were challenged, stretched, and pulled to places that would have broken anyone else. I searched my whole career for a business partner, and I found a phenomenal one in Sue. Our business partnership is a once-in-a-lifetime gift and is made even that much more special because of our relationship as sisters!

Finally, I would like to thank the Universe for inspiring, nagging, and insisting on a cold, dreary February day in Chicago that I spend it hand-writing all of *Founderology*. The message of the book came to me that day—to write for the purposes of creating unity, harmony, and alignment in the workplace. There has never been a more important time than right now for **everyone** to find positive and productive ways to work **together** in transforming visions to reality!

About the Author

KATHLEEN WOOD

Founder/CEO of Kathleen Wood Partners and Suzy's Swirl

Kathleen Wood knows Founders because she is a Founder. Kathleen founded her first company over twenty years ago, with her cleverly named growth strategy firm, Kathleen Wood Partners. Her firm specializes in strategic growth planning, business optimization, competitive brand development, and leadership development.

Kathleen Wood Partners works with Founders, entrepreneurs, and business owners with strategies to transform their visions into reality. Kathleen has consulted with Founders and Employees across the United States and internationally in the process of growing great companies, building high-performance teams, and award-winning brands.

In 2012, Kathleen co-founded Suzy's Swirl, an innovative frozen dessert company, with her business partner and sister, Sue Tierno, and her nieces, Jen and Julie. The brand features cool combinations of frozen yogurts, sorbettos, gelatos and so much more. Suzy's Swirl is on a mission to inspire *one million moments of frozen happiness, one cup at a time.*

Kathleen is a nationally recognized growth strategist, motivational speaker, author, and proven leader in building businesses and nonprofits. Kathleen has been recognized for her work in numerous publications and podcasts. In 2010, she published her first book, *The Best Shift of Your Life: The Restaurant Manager's Guide for Success Outside the Restaurant.*

Kathleen energetically lives her life as a Founder, enjoying and being inspired by all the possibilities of the world!

kwoodpartners.com

suzysswirl.com

Contact Kathleen Wood

KWoodPartners.com

Kathleen@KWoodPartners.com

Facebook.com/KathleenWoodPartners

Instagram.com/KWoodPartners

Linkedin.com/in/KathleenWoodPartners

Tag Us
#Founderology
#EmployeeEngagement
#Entreprenuers
#TeamPerformance
#BusinessSuccess

The *Founderology* Employee
One Page Success Plan